The Writer's Wo...
Paragraph Patterns
and the Essay

Lynne Gaetz
Lionel Groulx College

Suneeti Phadke
St. Jerome College

PEARSON
Prentice Hall

Upper Saddle River, New Jersey 07458

Library of Congress Cataloging-in-Publication Data

Gaetz, Lynne
The Writer's World: paragraph patterns and the essay / Lynne Gaetz, Suneeti Phadke.
    p. cm.
Includes index.
ISBN 0-13-172769-9
    1. English language—Paragraphs—Problems, exercises, etc.   2. English
language—Rhetoric—Problems, exercises, etc.   3. English language—Grammar—Problems,
exercises, etc.   4. English language—Textbooks for foreign speakers. 5. Report writing—
Problems, exercises, etc.   I. Phadke, Suneeti   II. Title.

PE1439.G26 2006
808'.042—dc22   2005047633

Editorial Director: Leah Jewell
Executive Editor: Craig Campanella
Acquisitions Assistant: Joan Polk
VP/Director, Production and Manufacturing: Barbara Kittle
Production Editor: Joan E. Foley
Production Assistant: Marlene Gassler
Copyeditor: Kathryn Graehl
Text Permissions Specialist: Jane Scelta
Development Editor in Chief: Rochelle Diogenes
Development Editor: Veronica Tomaiuolo
Manufacturing Manager: Nick Sklitsis
Prepress and Manufacturing Buyer: Benjamin Smith
VP/Director, Marketing: Brandy Dawson
Marketing Manager: Kate Mitchell
Marketing Assistant: Anthony DeCosta

Media Project Manager: Alison Lorber
Director, Image Resource Center: Melinda Reo
Manager, Image Rights and Permissions: Zina Arabia
Manager, Visual Research: Beth Brenzel
Image Permissions Coordinator: Frances Toepfer
Image Researcher: Sheila Norman
Manager, Cover Visual Research & Permissions: Karen Sanatar
Director, Creative Design: Leslie Osher
Art Director, Interior Design: Laura Gardner
Cover Design: Anne DeMarinis
Cover Art: (front) Judith Miller Archive/Dorling Kindersley Media Library; (rear) Photodisc Green/Getty Images, Inc.; Brand X Pictures/Getty Images, Inc.; Royalty Free/CORBIS; Stockdisc Classice/Getty Images, Inc.

This book was set in 11/13 Janson by Pine Tree Composition, Inc., and was printed and bound by Courier Companies, Inc. Covers were printed by Phoenix Color Corp.

PEARSON EDUCATION LTD.
PEARSON EDUCATION SINGAPORE, PTE. LTD
PEARSON EDUCATION, CANADA, LTD
PEARSON EDUCATION–JAPAN
PEARSON EDUCATION AUSTRALIA PTY, LIMITED

PEARSON EDUCATION NORTH ASIA LTD
PEARSON EDUCACIÓN DE MEXICO, S.A. DE C.V.
PEARSON EDUCATION MALAYSIA, PTE. LTD
PEARSON EDUCATION, UPPER SADDLE RIVER, NJ

10 9 8 7 6 5 4 3 2

ISBN 0-13-172769-9

Contents

PART II — Paragraph Patterns 52

 Illustration 53

 Narration 64

Description 76

 **Process** 88

Definition 100

 Classification 113

Comparison and Contrast 126

 Cause and Effect 140

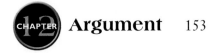 **Argument** 153

 The Essay 168

 Writing the Essay 169

 Essay Patterns 193

Enhancing Your Writing with Research 237

Appendices

About the Individual Volumes of *The Writer's World: Paragraphs and Essays*

Prentice Hall is proud to offer *The Writer's World: Paragraphs and Essays* in four individual volumes—all created directly from the pages of the parent text by Lynne Gaetz and Suneeti Phadke:

- *The Writer's World: Writing Process* (Part I, Chapters 1-3)
- *The Writer's World: Paragraph Patterns and the Essay* (Parts II-III, Chapters 4-15)
- *The Writer's World: Editing Handbook* (Part IV, Chapters 16-36)
- *The Writer's World: Reading Strategies and Selections* (Part V, Chapter 37)

Instructors teach writing in different ways. Developed for maximum flexibility, *The Writer's World* volumes help instructors tailor courses to their specific needs. For example, instructors who prefer using their own reading selections may choose only the first three volumes. Other instructors may want to take advantage of only thematic grammar, so they might choose only the third volume.

Other features of *The Writer's World* individual volumes include:

Value: Each volume sells at a price significantly less than the parent text. This value pricing allows instructors who require three or fewer volumes for the course to give students the option of purchasing only the volumes they need to fulfill course requirements.

Page Numbers: The page numbers remain consistent with the page numbers in the parent text. As a result, an instructor using the Annotated Instructor's Edition can easily work with an entire class regardless of which students are using individual volumes and which are using the parent text.

Links: The parent text contains margin references (Writing Links, Reading Links, and Grammar Links) that connect material to other parts of the book. Since students using only individual volumes will not have access to all of the linked pages, we have eliminated some links from these books.

Resources: *The Writer's World* has a rich collection of resources for college adopters of both the parent text and the individual volumes. Any two of the following supplements may be packaged with a volume at no additional cost:

- The Visualizing Writing CD-ROM (ISBN: 0-13-194108-9)
- The Prentice Hall Grammar Workbook, Second Edition (0-13-194771-0)
- The Prentice Hall Editing Workbook (0-13-189352-1)
- Applying English to Your Career (0-13-192115-0)
- The Prentice Hall ESL Workbook, Second Edition (0-13-194759-1)
- The Prentice Hall Writer's Journal (0-13-184900-X)
- *The New American Webster Handy College Dictionary* (0-13-045258-0)
- *The New American Roget's College Thesaurus* (0-13-045258-0)

Many more packaging options are available. For a complete listing, please contact your local Prentice Hall representative.

About the First Edition of *The Writer's World: Paragraph Patterns and the Essay*

Whether your students enroll in the course with varying skill levels, whether they are native or nonnative speakers of English, or whether they learn better through the use of visuals, *The Writer's World* can help students produce writing that is technically correct and rich in content. It is our goal for this preface to give you a deeper understanding of how we arranged the text and the key components found in *The Writer's World: Paragraphs and Essays*.

A Research-Based Approach

From the onset of the development process, we have comprehensively researched the needs and desires of current developmental writing instructors. We met with more than 45 instructors from around the country, asking for their opinions and insights regarding (1) the challenges posed by the course, (2) the needs of today's ever-changing student population, and (3) the ideas and features we were proposing in order to provide them and you with a more effective learning and teaching tool. Prentice Hall also commissioned dozens of detailed manuscript reviews from instructors, asking them to analyze and evaluate each draft of the manuscript. These reviewers identified numerous ways in which we could refine and enhance our key features. Their invaluable feedback was incorporated throughout *The Writer's World*. The text you are seeing is truly the product of a successful partnership between the authors, publisher, and well over 100 developmental writing instructors.

How We Organized *The Writer's World*

Part II: Paragraph Patterns gives students a solid overview of the patterns of development. Using the same easy-to-understand process (Exploring, Developing, and Revising and Editing), each chapter in this section explains how to convey ideas using one or more writing patterns. As they work through the practices and write their own paragraphs and essays, students begin to see how using a writing pattern can help them fulfill their purpose for writing.

Part III: The Essay covers the parts of the essay and explains how students can apply the nine patterns of development to essay writing. This section also discusses the role research plays in writing and explains some ways that students can incorporate research in their essays.

How *The Writer's World* Meets Students' Diverse Needs

We created *The Writer's World* to meet your students' diverse needs. To accomplish this, we asked both the instructors in our focus groups and the reviewers at every stage not only to critique our ideas but to offer their suggestions and recommendations for features that would enhance the learning process of their students. The result

has been the integration of many elements that are not found in other textbooks, including our visual program, coverage of nonnative speaker material, and strategies for addressing the varying skill levels students bring to the course.

The Visual Program

A stimulating, full-color book, *The Writer's World* recognizes that today's world is a visual one, and it encourages students to become better communicators by responding to images. Chapter opening visuals in Parts II and III help students to think about the chapter's key concepts in new ways. For example, in the Chapter 9 opener, a photograph of a car lot sets the stage for classification. Cars are grouped according to their models and makes, which helps students understand the premise of classification.

Each **At Work** box in Part II features an image from the workplace, along with content on how that particular pattern of development is utilized on the job.

Seamless Coverage for Nonnative Speakers

Instructors in our focus groups noted the growing number of nonnative/ESL speakers enrolling in the developmental writing courses. Although some of these students have special needs relating to the writing process, many of you still have a large portion of native speakers in your courses whose more traditional needs must also be satisfied. To meet the challenge of this rapidly changing dynamic, we have carefully implemented and integrated content throughout to assist these students. *The Writer's World* does not have separate ESL boxes, ESL chapters, or tacked-on ESL appendices. Instead, information that traditionally poses challenges to nonnative speakers is woven seamlessly throughout the book. In our extensive experience teaching writing to both native and nonnative speakers of English, we have learned that both groups learn best when they are not distracted by ESL labels. With the seamless approach, nonnative speakers do not feel self-conscious and segregated, and native speakers do not tune out to detailed explanations that may also benefit them. Many of these traditional problem areas receive more coverage than you would find in other textbooks, arming the instructor with the material to effectively meet the needs of nonnative speakers.

What Tools Can Help Students Get the Most from *The Writer's World*?

Overwhelmingly, focus group participants and reviewers asked that both a larger number and a greater diversity of exercises and activities be incorporated into a new text. In response to this feedback, we have developed and tested the following items in *The Writer's World*. These tools form the pedagogical backbone of the book, and we are confident they will help your students become better writers.

Hints

In each chapter, **Hint** boxes highlight important writing and grammar points. Hints are useful for all students, but many will be particularly helpful for nonnative speakers. For example, in Chapter 12 there is a hint about being direct and avoiding circular reasoning.

The Writer's Desk

Parts II and III include **The Writer's Desk** exercises that help students get used to practicing all stages and steps of the writing process. Students begin with prewriting and then progress to developing, organizing (using paragraph and essay plans), drafting, and finally, revising and editing to create a final draft.

Paragraph Patterns "At Work"

To help students appreciate the relevance of their writing tasks, Chapters 4-12 begin with an authentic writing sample. Titled **Illustration at Work, Narration at Work,** and so on, this feature offers a glimpse of the writing patterns people use in different types of workplace writing.

Reflect On It

Each **Reflect On It** is a chapter review exercise. Questions prompt students to recall and review what they have learned in the chapter.

The Writer's Room

The Writer's Room contains writing activities that correspond to general, college, and workplace topics. Some prompts are brief to allow students to freely form ideas while others are expanded to give students more direction.

There is literally something for every student writer in this end-of-chapter feature. Students who respond well to visual cues will appreciate the photo writing exercises in **The Writer's Room** in Part II: Paragraph Patterns. Students who learn best by hearing through collaboration will appreciate the discussion and group work prompts in **The Writers' Circle** section of selected **The Writer's Rooms.** In Part III: The Essay, students can respond to thought-provoking quotations.

Acknowledgments

Many people have helped us produce *The Writer's World*. First and foremost, we would like to thank our students for inspiring us and providing us with extraordinary feedback. Their words and insights pervade this book.

We also benefited greatly from the insightful comments and suggestions from over 200 instructors across the nation, all of whom are listed in the opening pages of the Annotated Instructor's Edition. Our colleagues' feedback was invaluable and helped shape *The Writer's World* series content, focus, and organization.

We are indebted to the team of dedicated professionals at Prentice Hall who have helped make this project a reality. They have boosted our spirits and have believed in us every step of the way. Special thanks to Veronica Tomaiuolo for her magnificent job in polishing this book and to Craig Campanella for trusting our instincts and enthusiastically propelling us forward. Kate Mitchell worked tirelessly to ensure we were always meeting the needs of instructors. We owe a deep debt of gratitude to Yolanda de Rooy, whose encouraging words helped ignite this project. Joan Foley's attention to detail in the production process kept us motivated and on task and made *The Writer's World* a much better resource for both instructors and students. We would also like to thank Laura Gardner for her brilliant design, which helped keep the visual learner in all of us engaged.

Finally, we would like to dedicate this book to our husbands and children who supported us and who patiently put up with our long hours on the computer. Manu, Octavio, and Natalia continually encouraged us. We especially appreciate the help and sacrifices of Diego, Becky, Kiran, and Meghana.

Lynne Gaetz and family in Mexico

A Note to Students

Your knowledge, ideas, and opinions are important. The ability to clearly communicate those ideas is invaluable in your personal, academic, and professional life. When your writing is error-free, readers will focus on your message, and you will be able to persuade, inform, entertain, or inspire them. *The Writer's World* includes strategies that will help you improve your written communication. Quite simply, when you become a better writer, you become a better communicator. It is our greatest wish for *The Writer's World* to make you excited about writing, communicating, and learning.

Enjoy!
Lynne Gaetz and Suneeti Phadke
TheWritersWorld@hotmail.com

Suneeti Phadke and family in Quebec, Canada

PART II

Paragraph Patterns

What Is a Paragraph Pattern?

A *pattern* or *mode* is a method used to express one of the three purposes: to inform, to persuade, or to entertain. Once you know your purpose, you will be able to choose which writing pattern or patterns can help you to express it.

Patterns can overlap, and it is possible to use more than one pattern in a single piece of writing. For example, imagine you are writing a paragraph about bullying, and your purpose is to inform the reader. You might use *definition* as your predominant pattern but, in the supporting details, you might use *comparison and contrast* to compare a bully and a victim. You might also use *narration* to highlight an incident in which a bully harassed a victim.

Before you work through the next chapters, review the paragraph patterns.

Illustration
To illustrate or prove a point using specific examples

Narration
To narrate or tell a story about a sequence of events that happened

Process
To inform the reader about how to do something, how something works, or how something happened

Description
To describe using vivid details and images that appeal to the reader's senses

Definition
To define or explain what a term or concept means by providing relevant examples

Classification
To classify or sort a topic to help readers understand different qualities about that topic

Comparison and contrast
To present information about similarities (compare) or differences (contrast)

Cause and effect
To explain why an event happened (the cause) or what the consequences of the event were (the effects)

Argument*
To argue or to take a position on an issue and offer reasons for your position

*Argument is included as one of the nine patterns, but it is also a purpose in writing.

Illustration

> *A wisely chosen illustration is essential to fasten the truth upon the ordinary mind.*
>
> —HOWARD CROSBY
> *American preacher and educator (1826–1891)*

Vendors offer many examples of a product to interest consumers and to make a sale. In illustration writing, you give examples to support your point.

EXPLORING

Explore Topics

In the Warm Up, you will try an exploring strategy to generate ideas about different topics.

The Writer's Desk **Warm Up**

Think about the following questions, and write the first ideas that come to your mind. Try to think of two to three ideas for each topic.

EXAMPLE: What do students learn during the first week of college?

—how to find their way around campus (where is the computer lab, etc.?)

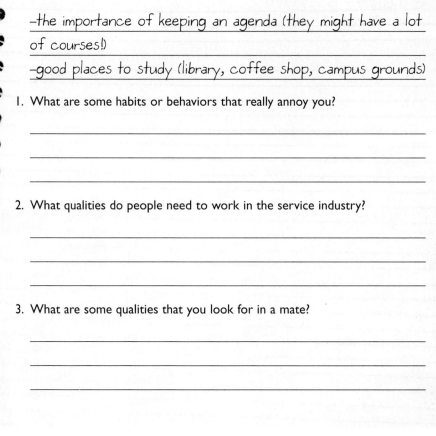

—the importance of keeping an agenda (they might have a lot of courses!)

—good places to study (library, coffee shop, campus grounds)

1. What are some habits or behaviors that really annoy you?

2. What qualities do people need to work in the service industry?

3. What are some qualities that you look for in a mate?

What Is Illustration?

When you write using **illustration,** you include specific examples to clarify your main point. You illustrate or give examples anytime you want to explain, analyze, narrate, or give an opinion about something. As a writer, you can use many different types of examples to help your reader acquire a deeper and clearer understanding of your subject. You can include personal experience or factual information, such as a statistic.

You give examples every day. When telling a friend why you had a good day or a bad day, you might use examples to make your story more interesting. At college, you might give an oral presentation using examples that will help your audience better understand your point. At work, you might give examples to show clients where or how they might market their products.

ESSAY LINK

You can develop illustration essays with a series of examples or extended examples.

The Illustration Paragraph

There are two ways to write an illustration paragraph.

- **Use a series of examples** to illustrate your main point. For example, if you are writing a paragraph about an innovative teacher that you had, you might list things that the teacher did, such as wear a costume, let students teach parts of the course, and use music to make a point.
- **Use an extended example** to illustrate your main point. The example can be an anecdote or a description of an event. For example, if you are writing about a stressful vacation, you might describe what happened when you lost your wallet.

The following *Illustration at Work* paragraph illustrates using a series of examples.

Illustration at Work

Patti Guzman is a registered nurse at a large hospital. She was invited to speak to nursing students in a local university. In the following excerpt from her speech, she gives examples to explain why a nurse must be in good physical health.

Physically, the job of a nurse is demanding. On a daily basis, we must lift patients and move them. When patients are bedridden for prolonged periods, we must change their positions on their beds. When new patients arrive, we transfer them from stretchers to beds or from beds to wheelchairs. If patients fall, we must be able to help them stand up. If patients have difficulty walking, we must assist them. Patients who have suffered paralysis or stroke need to be lifted and supported when they are bathed and dressed. Keep in mind that some patients may be quite heavy, so the job requires a good level of physical strength.

PRACTICE I

Read the next paragraph and answer the questions.

Across the country, lawmakers are coming up with inventive ways to punish criminals. Some judges in New Orleans, for example, treat offenders like unruly children. In 2003, one of the judges ordered a shoplifter in Baton Rouge to stand in front of a Dillard's store holding a sign that says "I will not shoplift anymore," and another judge ordered an offender to write "I will not steal other people's property" 2,500 times. In Florida, a hardworking judge orders drunk drivers to put bumper stickers on their cars that read, "How's my driving? The judge wants to know." The stickers feature a toll-free number. A Kentucky judge sometimes instructs **deadbeat dads** to choose between jail or a **vasectomy.** The best creative sentencing is done by a judge from Santa Fe, New Mexico. Judge Frances Gallegos, arguing that traditional anger management courses are ineffective, sentences violent offenders to tai chi, meditation, and Japanese flower-arranging classes.

—Rebecca Bloom, student

deadbeat dad: a father who avoids paying for his child's upkeep

vasectomy: medical procedure to sterilize a male

1. Underline the topic sentence of this paragraph. (The topic sentence expresses the main idea of the paragraph.)

2. What type of illustration paragraph is this? Circle the best answer.

   a. Series of examples   b. Extended example

3. List the examples that the writer gives to illustrate her point.

   _____

   _____

   _____

   _____

   _____

   _____

PRACTICE 2

Read the next paragraph and answer the questions.

> If there is a single trait that most distinguishes entrepreneurs, it is this: they have an uncanny ability to anticipate and supply what large numbers of people want. For example, here's how Akio Morita, the legendary founder of Sony, got his idea for the Sony Walkman. He would go to the beach with his children, and the kids and their friends would listen to high-volume ghetto blasters from morning to evening. Morita asked himself, "Why should I have to listen to this **ghastly** music?" And he wondered, "Why should they have to carry those **cumbersome** machines?" Morita told his engineers to figure out a way to build a small radio and cassette player that would sound like a high-quality car stereo and yet could be attached to a person's head. They obliged, and the Sony Walkman stormed the market.

—Dinesh D'Souza, "Billionaires," *Business 2.0*

ghastly: terrible

cumbersome: large and heavy

1. Underline the topic sentence.

2. What does the writer use to present his supporting details? Circle the best answer.

   a. a series of examples   b. an extended example

3. What example(s) does the writer give to illustrate his point? _____

   _____

4. What are the main events in the narrative? List them.

   _____

   _____

   _____

   _____

   _____

   _____

DEVELOPING

The Topic Sentence

The topic sentence of the illustration paragraph is a general statement that expresses both your topic and your controlling idea. To determine your controlling idea, think about what point you want to make.

topic   controlling idea
During my first months as a reporter, <u>I was often surprised at</u>
<u>people's behavior.</u>

controlling idea   topic
<u>Our father became anxious</u> **when my sister started dating.**

The Writer's Desk **Write Topic Sentences**

Write a topic sentence for each of the following topics. You can look for ideas in the Warm Up on pages 53–54. Each topic sentence should contain a general statement that expresses both your topic and your controlling idea.

EXAMPLE:

Topic: Lessons during the first week of college

Topic sentence: *During the first week of college, students learn valuable information about campus life.*

1. Topic: Things that are annoying

   Topic sentence: _____

   _____

2. Topic: Qualities people need to work in the service industry

   Topic sentence: _____

   _____

3. Topic: Qualities in a mate

   Topic sentence: _____

   _____

ESSAY LINK

In an illustration essay, the thesis statement expresses the controlling idea.

The Supporting Ideas

After you have developed an effective topic sentence, generate supporting ideas. In an illustration paragraph, you can give a series of examples or an extended example.

When you use a series of examples, you can arrange your examples in emphatic order. Emphatic order means that you can place your examples from the most to the least important or from the least to the most important. If you use an extended example, you can arrange your ideas using time order.

The Writer's Desk **Generate Supporting Ideas**

Generate some supporting examples under each topic. Make sure your examples support the topic sentences that you wrote for the previous Writer's Desk.

EXAMPLE: Lessons during the first week of college

when the sports complex opens

clubs on campus

where is the library

good instructors

1. Things that annoy you

_____

_____

_____

_____

2. Qualities needed to work in the service industry

_____

_____

_____

_____

3. Qualities you look for in a mate

_____

_____

_____

_____

ESSAY LINK

In an illustration essay, place the thesis statement in the introduction. Then, structure the essay so that each supporting idea becomes a distinct paragraph with its own topic sentence.

The Paragraph Plan

A paragraph plan helps you organize your topic sentence and supporting details before writing a first draft. When you write a paragraph plan, ensure that your examples are valid and relate to the topic sentence. Also include details that will help clarify your supporting examples. Organize your ideas in a logical order.

TOPIC SENTENCE: <u>During the first week of college, students learn valuable information about campus life.</u>

Support 1: They learn how to find their way around campus.

Details: —locations of classrooms and instructors' offices

Support 2:	They get information about the personalities of instructors.
Details:	—nice versus strict instructors
Support 3:	They find good places to eat.
Details:	—try cafeteria food
	—find out if there are coffee shops or fast-food outlets on campus
Support 4:	They discover the availability of computers.
Details:	—computer lab opening hours
	—lab technician availability

The Writer's Desk **Write a Paragraph Plan**

Choose one of the topic sentences that you wrote for the Writer's Desk on page 57. Write a paragraph plan using some of the supporting ideas that you have generated. Include details for each supporting idea.

Topic sentence: _____

_____

Support 1: _____

Details: _____

_____

Support 2: _____

Details: _____

_____

Support 3: _____

Details: _____

_____

Support 4: _____

Details: _____

_____

The First Draft

After you outline your ideas in a plan, you are ready to write the first draft. Remember to write complete sentences. You might include transitional words or expressions to help your ideas flow smoothly.

Transitional Words and Expressions

Transitional expressions can help you introduce an example or show an additional example. The next transitional words are useful in illustration paragraphs.

To Introduce an Example		To Show an Additional Example	
for example	namely	also	in addition
for instance	specifically	first (second, etc.)	in another case
in other words	to illustrate	furthermore	moreover

The Writer's Desk **Write the First Draft**

In the previous Writer's Desk, you developed a paragraph plan. Now write the first draft of your illustration paragraph. Before you write, carefully review your paragraph plan and make any necessary changes.

REVISING AND EDITING

Revise and Edit an Illustration Paragraph

When you finish writing an illustration paragraph, review your work and revise it to make the example(s) as clear as possible to your readers. Check to make sure that the order of ideas is logical, and remove any irrelevant details. Before you work on your own paragraph, practice revising and editing a student paragraph.

PRACTICE 3

Read the next student paragraph and answer the questions.

During the first week of college, students learn valuable information about campus life. First, new students learn how to find your way around campus. They discover the location of the classrooms and the instructors' offices. Furthermore, they learn about the personalities of their instructors. Perhaps one instructor is strict, another is easygoing. Students often gossip on campus. In the first week, students also learn about good places to study. For example, many students like to work in the library because it is peaceful. Some also study in the campus coffee shop. On the other hand, the cafeteria may be noisy and is not a good place to study. Basically, it is important to find out how the campus functions early in the semester.

Revising

1. Highlight the topic sentence in this paragraph.

2. List the examples that illustrate the topic sentence.

_____

_____

_____

3. This paragraph lacks unity, and one sentence is not relevant. Cross it out.

Editing

4. There is a pronoun error in the paragraph: one pronoun does not agree with its antecedent. Identify the incorrect sentence. Then write the correct sentence in the space below.

Correction: _____

_____

5. This paragraph contains a type of run-on sentence called a comma splice. Two complete sentences are incorrectly connected with a comma. Identify the incorrect sentence. Then correct it in the space below.

Correction: _____

_____

The Writer's Desk **Revise and Edit Your Paragraph**

Revise and edit the paragraph that you wrote for the Writer's Desk on page 60. Ensure that your paragraph has unity, adequate support, and coherence. Also, correct any errors in grammar, spelling, punctuation, and mechanics.

REFLECT ON IT

Think about what you have learned in this chapter. If you do not know an answer, review that topic.

1. In an illustration paragraph, you _____

2. There are two ways to write illustration paragraphs. Explain each of them.

   a. Using a series of examples: _____

   b. Using an extended example: _____

   _____

3. List three transitional expressions that indicate an additional idea.

   _____

   _____

   _____

 *The Writer's Room* **Topics for Illustration Paragraphs**

Writing Activity I

Choose any of the following topics, or choose your own topic. Then write an illustration paragraph.

General Topics

1. ridiculous fads or fashions
2. good or bad habits
3. punishment for crimes
4. activities that relieve stress
5. possible future inventions
6. the consequences of losing your temper

College and Work-Related Topics

7. items that every student needs
8. qualities that can help you succeed
9. comfortable work clothes
10. reasons for working
11. tools or equipment needed for your job
12. qualities of a good boss

Writing Activity 2

The image depicts a man who feels like he is walking on a tightrope, and the image expresses anxiety. What things make you feel worried? Write an illustration paragraph about things that make you feel worried or stressed.

 ILLUSTRATION PARAGRAPH CHECKLIST

After you write your illustration paragraph, review the checklist on the inside front cover. Also ask yourself the following questions.

Does my topic sentence make a point that can be supported with examples?

Does my paragraph contain sufficient examples that clearly support the topic sentence?

Do I use transitions to smoothly connect my examples?

Have I arranged my examples in a logical order?

CHAPTER 5

Narration

> *It's all storytelling, you know. That's what journalism is all about.*
>
> —TOM BROKAW
> *American broadcast journalist (b. 1940)*

When investigating a crime scene, a detective must try to find answers to the questions who, what, when, where, why, and how. You answer the same questions when you write a narrative paragraph.

EXPLORING

Explore Topics

In the Warm Up, you will try an exploring strategy to generate ideas about different topics.

The Writer's Desk **Warm Up**

Think about the following questions, and write down the first ideas that come to your mind. Try to think of two or three ideas for each topic.

EXAMPLE: What interesting stories have family members told you about their lives?

My dad's story about his arrival in this country—funny story about his first job. Uncle Pancho likes to talk about when he bought some land. The day my sister won a piano competition (she's annoying). What else? When my mom met my dad.

1. What are some serious decisions that you have made? Think about decisions relating to school, personal relationships, work, and so on.

_____

_____

_____

2. What experiences have you had that have changed you in some way?

_____

_____

_____

3. What are some funny things that you have seen? List some amusing stories.

_____

_____

_____

What Is Narration?

When you **narrate,** you tell a story about what happened. You generally explain events in the order in which they occurred, and you include information about when they happened and who was involved in the incidents.

You use narration every day. You may write about the week's events in your personal journal, or you might send a postcard to a friend detailing what you did during your vacation. At college, you may explain what happened during a historical event or what happened in a novel that you have read. At work, you might use narration to explain an incident involving a customer or co-worker.

Narration is not only useful on its own; it also enhances other types of writing. For example, Jason must write an argument essay about youth crime. His essay will be more compelling if he includes a personal anecdote about the time a gang of youths attacked him in a subway station. In other words, narration can provide supporting evidence for other essay patterns.

The Narrative Paragraph

There are two main types of narrative paragraphs.

1. **Use first-person narration (autobiography).**
In first-person narration, you describe a personal experience from your point of view. You are directly involved in the story. You use the words *I* (first-

ESSAY LINK

In a narrative essay, you can use first- or third-person narration.

person singular) or *we* (first-person plural). For example: "When I was a child, I thought that the world began and ended with me. I didn't know, or care, how other children felt. Thus, when schoolmates ridiculed a shy boy, I gleefully joined in." The *Narration at Work* paragraph on this page is an example of first-person narration.

2. Use third-person narration.

In third-person narration, you do not refer to your own experiences. Instead, you describe what happened to somebody else. The story is told in the third person using *he, she, it,* or *they*. You might tell a story about your mother's childhood, or you might explain what happened during the last election. In this type of narration, you are simply an observer or storyteller; you are not a participant in the action. For example: "The students gathered to protest against the war. One student threw a chair through the window of the student center. Suddenly, people started pushing and shoving."

Hint   Choose an Interesting Topic

When you write a narrative paragraph, try to choose a topic that will interest the reader. For example, the reader might not be interested if you write about the act of eating your lunch. However, if you write about a time when your best friend argued with a waiter during a meal, you could create an entertaining narrative paragraph.

Think about a topic that you personally find very interesting, and then share it with your readers.

Narration at Work

Joseph Roth, a boiler and pressure vessel inspector, used narrative writing in a memo he wrote to his supervisor.

As you know, I recently inspected the boiler and pressure vessels in the refinery on Highway 11. I had a few problems that I would like to mention. When I first arrived, the manager of the unit was uncooperative and initially tried to stop me from examining the boiler! After much discussion, I was finally permitted into the boiler room where I noticed several defects in the operation and condition of the equipment. Immediately, I saw that the low-water fuel cut-off chamber was filled with sludge and could not possibly function properly. Then I realized that the boiler heating surfaces were covered with scale. Finally, I found stress cracks in the tube ends and in tube seats. This is a sure sign of caustic imbrittlement, making the boiler unsafe to operate and in danger of exploding. I have asked that the boiler be taken out of service immediately.

We must follow up to make sure that measures are being taken to replace the boiler.

PRACTICE I

The author of the next paragraph was born in 1876 and was raised on the Pine Ridge Reservation in South Dakota. At the age of twelve, she was sent to a Quaker missionary school. Read the paragraph and answer the questions.

There were eight in our party of bronzed children who were going East with the missionaries. We had anticipated much pleasure from a ride on the train, but the **throngs** of staring palefaces disturbed and troubled us. Fair women, with tottering babies on each arm, stopped their haste and **scrutinized** the children of absent mothers. Large men, with heavy bundles in their hands, halted nearby, and **riveted** their glassy blue eyes upon us. I sank deep into the corner of my seat, for I resented being watched. Directly in front of me, children who were no larger than I hung themselves upon the backs of their seats, with their bold white faces toward me. Sometimes they took their forefingers out of their mouths and pointed at my moccasined feet. Their mothers, instead of **reproving** such rude curiosity, looked closely at me, and attracted their children's further notice to my blanket. This embarrassed me, and kept me constantly on the verge of tears.

—Sitkala Sa, *Impressions of an Indian Childhood* (1900)

throngs: crowd or group

scrutinized: examined in detail

riveted: concentrated; focused intently

reproving: criticizing severely

1. Underline the topic sentence of this paragraph. (Remember, the topic sentence is not always the first sentence.)

2. What type of narration is this? Circle the best answer.
   a. First person   b. Third person

3. Who or what is the paragraph about? _____

   _____

4. In a few words, explain what happened in this paragraph. _____

   _____

5. When did it happen? _____

6. Where did it happen? _____

7. By combining your answers to questions 3 through 6, write a one-sentence summary of the paragraph. Someone who has never read the paragraph should have a clear idea of the paragraph's content after reading your sentence.

   _____

   _____

   _____

PRACTICE 2

Read the next paragraph and answer the questions.

The 1960s was a decade of profound social upheaval. The period began with optimism and excitement, as the young and charismatic John F. Kennedy was elected president of the United States. Idealistic civil rights workers, both black and white, sought to increase registration of black voters in the South and end housing discrimination in the North. The Reverend Dr. Martin Luther King attracted nationwide attention as he fought with **unprecedented** success (and immense dignity) to end segregation and racism in America without the use of violence. Soon, however, the idealism and optimism were shattered. President Kennedy was assassinated in 1963. The passage of the Civil Rights Act in 1965 was regarded by many new militant black groups as "too little, too late." Riots broke out in many cities in the summers of 1965–68. In 1968, both Martin Luther King and Robert Kennedy, the president's brother, were gunned down. But the most divisive force in American society in the 1960s was the Vietnam War.

—Jeremy Yudkin, *Understanding Music*

unprecedented: something that never happened before; without precedent

1. Who or what is the paragraph about? _____

2. Underline the topic sentence of this paragraph.

3. What type of narration is this? Circle the best answer.
   a. First person   b. Third person

4. How does the writer support the topic sentence? List the smaller events that make up this narrative.

   _____

   _____

   _____

   _____

   _____

   _____

   _____

5. Do the supporting facts provide adequate support for the topic sentence?

   _____

ESSAY LINK

In a narrative essay, the thesis statement expresses the controlling idea.

DEVELOPING

The Topic Sentence

When you write a narrative paragraph, it is important to express a main point. If you simply describe a list of activities, it is boring for the reader. To make your paragraph interesting, make sure that your topic sentence has a controlling idea.

topic　　　　　　　　controlling idea
When somebody broke into my house, <u>I felt totally invaded.</u>

controlling idea　　　　topic
<u>I learned to be responsible</u> **during my first job.**

> ⬭ **Hint**   **Make a Point**
>
> In a narrative paragraph, the topic sentence should make a point. To help you find the controlling idea, you can ask yourself the following questions.
>
> • What did I learn?　　　　　• How did it make me feel?
>
> • How did I change?　　　　　• What is important about it?
>
> **Example:**
>
> Topic:　　　　　　　　　　*Moving out of the family home*
>
> Possible controlling idea:　*Becoming more independent*
>
> 　　　　　　　topic　　　　　　　　　controlling idea
> **When I moved out of the family home,** <u>I became more independent.</u>

PRACTICE 3

Practice writing topic sentences. Complete the following sentences by adding a controlling idea.

1. When I moved out of the family home, I felt (or I will feel) _____

 _____

2. In my first job, I learned _____

 _____

3. When I read _____, I realized _____

 _____

The Writer's Desk Write Topic Sentences

Write a topic sentence for each of the following topics. You can look for ideas in the Warm Up on page 64. Each topic sentence should mention the topic and express a controlling idea.

EXAMPLE:

Topic: A family story

Topic sentence:　*When my father found his first job in America, there was a humorous misunderstanding.*

1. Topic: A serious decision

   Topic sentence: _____

   _____

2. Topic: A life-changing event

   Topic sentence: _____

   _____

3. Topic: A funny story

   Topic sentence: _____

   _____

The Supporting Ideas

A narrative paragraph should contain specific details so that the reader understands what happened. To come up with the details, ask yourself a series of questions. Your paragraph should provide answers to these questions.

- Who is the paragraph about?
- What happened?
- When did it happen?
- Where did it happen?
- Why did it happen?
- How did it happen?

When you recount a story to a friend, you may go back and add details, saying, "I forgot to mention something." When you write a narrative paragraph, however, your sequence of events should be clearly chronological so that your reader can follow your story.

The Writer's Desk Develop Supporting Ideas

Generate supporting ideas for each topic. List what happened.

EXAMPLE: A family story   1. A serious decision

dad saw an ad   _____

"busboy" job   _____

bowling alley   _____

dad didn't understand ad   _____

man gave him a dishcloth   _____

2. A life-changing event   3. A funny story

_____   _____

_____   _____

_____   _____

_____   _____

_____   _____

The Paragraph Plan

Before you write a narrative paragraph, it is a good idea to make a paragraph plan. Write down main events in the order in which they occurred. To make your narration more complete, include details about each event.

ESSAY LINK

In a narrative essay, you place the thesis statement in the introduction. Each main event is developed in a supporting paragraph.

TOPIC SENTENCE:	When my father found his first job in America, there was a humorous misunderstanding.
Support 1:	—In a newspaper, he found an ad for a busboy.
Details:	—job was in a bowling alley
	—dad didn't speak English
Support 2:	—He went to the bowling alley.
Details:	—applied for the job, and got it
	—was excited
Support 3:	—On his first day, his boss asked him to put on an apron and told him to pick up some dishes in the bowling alley's restaurant.
Details:	—father was disappointed and asked, "Where's the bus?"
	—thought that a "busboy" would work on a bus

The Writer's Desk **Write a Paragraph Plan**

Choose one of the topic sentences that you wrote for the Writer's Desk on page 69. Write a paragraph plan using some of the supporting ideas that you have generated. Include details for each supporting idea.

Topic sentence: _____

_____

Support 1: _____

Details: _____

_____

_____

Support 2: _____

Details: _____

_____

_____

Support 3: _____

Details: _____

_____

_____

The First Draft

After you outline your ideas in a plan, you are ready to write the first draft. Remember to write complete sentences. You might include transitional words or expressions to help your ideas flow smoothly.

Transitional Words and Expressions

Transitions can help you show a sequence of events. The next transitional words are useful in narrative paragraphs.

To Show a Sequence of Events			
afterward	finally	in the end	meanwhile
after that	first	last	next
eventually	in the beginning	later	then

The Writer's Desk **Write the First Draft**

In the previous Writer's Desk, you developed a paragraph plan. Now write the first draft of your narrative paragraph. Before you write, carefully review your paragraph plan and make any necessary changes.

REVISING AND EDITING

Revise and Edit a Narrative Paragraph

When you finish writing a narrative paragraph, carefully review your work and revise it to make the events as clear as possible to your readers. Check that you have organized events chronologically, and remove any irrelevant details. Before you revise and edit your own paragraph, practice revising and editing a student paragraph.

PRACTICE 4

Read the next student paragraph and answer the questions.

When my father found his first job in America, there was a humorous misunderstanding. My father, originally from Mexico City, had just moved to Dallas, Texas, and he did not speak English. One day, he sees an ad for a busboy job. He wanted the job, so he called the number in the ad. Later that day, he went for an interview in a bowling alley. The restaurant manager spoke with my father and offered him the job. That night, my father went home feeling very excited. The next day, when he arrived for work, the manager gave him an apron and asked him to pick up some dishes in the bowling alley restaurant. My father, feeling confused and dissapointed, asked, "Where is the bus?" He thought that a busboy would work on a bus collecting tickets. The owner laught and explained what a busboy's job is. When my father told the family this story, everybody thought it was funny, but they were also proud of his perseverance because today he has a university degree and a good job.

Revising

1. Write down the two parts of the topic sentence.

          topic   +   controlling idea

_____

2. What type of order do the specific details follow? Circle the best answer.
   a. Space   b. Time
   c. Emphatic   d. No order

3. What are some transitional expressions that the author used?

_____

4. What type of narration is this?
   a. First person   b. Third person

Editing

5. This paragraph contains a tense inconsistency. The tense shifts for no apparent reason. Identify the incorrect sentence. Then write the correct sentence in the space below.

Correction: _____

_____

6. This paragraph contains two misspelled words. Identify and correct them.

    Misspelled words   **Corrections**

    _____   _____

    _____   _____

The Writer's Desk Revise and Edit Your Paragraph

Revise and edit the paragraph that you wrote for Writer's Desk: Write the First Draft on page 72. Ensure that your paragraph has unity, adequate support, and coherence. Also correct any errors in grammar, spelling, punctuation, and mechanics.

REFLECT ON IT

Think about what you have learned in this chapter. If you do not know an answer, review that topic.

1. In narrative writing, you _____

2. What are the differences between the two following types of narration?

    First person: _____

    _____

    Third person: _____

    _____

3. What are some questions that you should you ask yourself when you write a narrative paragraph?

    _____

4. What organizational method is commonly used in narrative paragraphs? Circle the best answer.

    a. Space order   b. Time order   c. Emphatic order

The Writer's Room   Topics for Narrative Paragraphs

Writing Activity 1

Choose any of the following topics, or choose your own topic. Then write a narrative paragraph.

General Topics

1. a proud moment
2. a risky adventure
3. a move to a new place
4. a surprising coincidence
5. a news event that affected you
6. a memorable family story

College and Work-Related Topics

7. a embarrassing incident at college or work
8. an inspiring teacher or instructor
9. a positive or negative job interview
10. a difficult co-worker
11. your best experience at work
12. your first job

Writing Activity 2

Have you ever lived through an earthquake, a tornado, a flood, a large storm, an extended power outage, or any other event caused by nature? What happened? What did you do? Write a narrative paragraph about a big storm or a natural event that you have lived through.

 NARRATIVE PARAGRAPH CHECKLIST

As you write your narrative paragraph, review the checklist on the inside front cover. Also ask yourself the following questions.

☐ Does my topic sentence clearly express the topic of the narration?

☐ Does my topic sentence contain a controlling idea that is meaningful and interesting?

☐ Does my paragraph answer most of the following questions: *who, what, when, where, why, how?*

☐ Do I use transitional expressions that help clarify the order of events?

☐ Do I include details to make my narration more interesting?

CHAPTER 6

Description

The beginning of human knowledge is through the senses, and the writer begins where human perception begins.

—FLANNERY O'CONNOR
American author (1925–1964)

A fine artist uses a variety of colors and brush strokes to make an impression on the viewer. In descriptive writing, you use words to create an image that your readers can visualize.

EXPLORING

Explore Topics

In the Warm Up, you will try an exploring strategy to generate ideas about different topics.

The Writer's Desk **Warm Up**

Think about the following questions, and write down the first ideas that come to your mind. Try to think of two or three ideas for each topic.

EXAMPLE: What are some useless products or other items that you own?

The plastic apple cutter (makes six perfect pieces). Never use it.
Useless toy called a Furby. As a kid, I used it a couple of times.
The juicer. It sits and collects dust.

1. What were some very emotional moments in your life? (Think about two or three moments when you felt extreme joy, sadness, excitement, anxiety, or other strong emotions.)

_____

_____

_____

2. Describe your food quirks. What are your unusual tastes or eating habits? Which foods do you really love or hate?

_____

_____

_____

3. What are some very busy places?

_____

_____

_____

What Is Description?

Description creates vivid images in the reader's mind by portraying people, places, or moments in detail.

You use description every day. At home, you might describe a new friend to your family, or you might describe an object that you bought. At college, you might describe the structure of a cell or the results of a lab experiment. At work, you may describe a new product to a client, or you could describe the qualities of potential clients to your boss. The *Description at Work* paragraph on the following page shows how one company used description in their brochure.

The Descriptive Paragraph

When you write a descriptive paragraph, focus on three main points.

1. **Create a dominant impression.**
   The dominant impression is the overall atmosphere that you wish to convey. It can be a strong feeling, mood, or image. For example, if you are describing a business meeting, you can emphasize the tension in the room.

ESSAY LINK

In descriptive essays, you should also create a dominant impression, express your attitude toward the subject, and include concrete details.

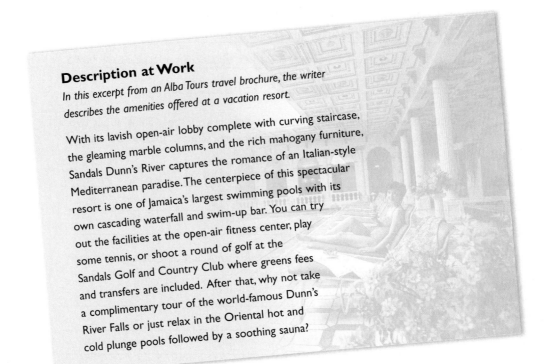

Description at Work

In this excerpt from an Alba Tours travel brochure, the writer describes the amenities offered at a vacation resort.

With its lavish open-air lobby complete with curving staircase, the gleaming marble columns, and the rich mahogany furniture, Sandals Dunn's River captures the romance of an Italian-style Mediterranean paradise. The centerpiece of this spectacular resort is one of Jamaica's largest swimming pools with its own cascading waterfall and swim-up bar. You can try out the facilities at the open-air fitness center, play some tennis, or shoot a round of golf at the Sandals Golf and Country Club where greens fees and transfers are included. After that, why not take a complimentary tour of the world-famous Dunn's River Falls or just relax in the Oriental hot and cold plunge pools followed by a soothing sauna?

2. **Express your attitude toward the subject.**

   Do you feel positive, negative, or neutral toward the subject? For example, if you feel positive about your best friend, then the details of your paragraph should convey the good feelings you have toward him or her. If you describe a place that you do not like, then your details should express how uncomfortable that place makes you feel. You might make a neutral description of a science lab experiment.

3. **Include concrete details.**

   Details will enable a reader to visualize the person, place, or situation that is being described. You can use active verbs and adjectives so that the reader imagines the scene more clearly. You can also use **imagery,** which is description using the five senses. Review the following examples of imagery.

Sight	At five-foot-nine, and a hundred and seventy-four pounds, I was muscularly inferior to the guys on the same athletic level and quite conscious of the fact.

   —H. D., "Dying to Be Bigger"

Sound	They hooked wrist-thick hanks of laghmien noodles and shoveled them into their mouths, slurping, sucking, inhaling, and chomping off portions. . . .

   —Jeffrey Tayler, "A Cacophony of Noodles"

Smell	For several days the wind blew, full of dust scents and the dryness of sagebrush, carrying eastward our own autumn smell of falling maple leaves, green walnuts, and the warm lemon odor of quince and yellow apples.

   —Josephine Johnson, "September Harvest"

Touch   My heart started racing, perspiration dripped down my face causing my glasses to slide, and I had a hard time breathing.

—Bebe Moore Campbell, "Dancing with Fear"

Taste   I asked for fresh lemonade, and got it—delicious, and cold, and tangy with real fruit.

—Mary Stewart, *My Brother Michael*

PRACTICE I

Read the next paragraph and answer the questions.

He had changed since his New Haven years. Now he was a sturdy straw-haired man of thirty with a rather hard mouth and a **supercilious** manner. Two shining arrogant eyes had established dominance over his face and gave him the appearance of always leaning aggressively forward. Not even the **effeminate swank** of his riding clothes could hide the enormous power of that body—he seemed to fill those glistening boots until he strained the top lacing, and you could see a great pack of muscle shifting when his shoulder moved under his thin coat. It was a body capable of enormous leverage—a cruel body.

—F. Scott Fitzgerald, *The Great Gatsby*

supercilious: arrogant

effeminate: having feminine qualities

swank: flashy appearance

1. What is the attitude of the writer toward the subject of the paragraph? Circle the best answer.

   a. Positive   b. Negative   c. Neutral

2. Write at least two examples that support your answer to question 1.

   _____

   _____

3. What is the dominant impression conveyed through this paragraph? Circle the best answer.

   a. Weakness   b. Laziness   c. Femininity   d. Strength

4. Write at least two examples from the text that show the dominant impression.

   _____

   _____

5. What sense is used to describe the character portrayed in this paragraph? Circle the best answer.

   a. Touch   b. Smell   c. Sight   d. Sound   e. Taste

6. Identify an example of imagery, and write it in the following spaces.

   _____

   _____

ESSAY LINK

In a descriptive essay, the thesis statement expresses the controlling idea.

DEVELOPING

When you write a descriptive paragraph, choose a subject that lends itself to description. In other words, find a subject to describe that appeals to the senses. For example, you can describe the sounds, sights, and smells in a bakery.

The Topic Sentence

In the topic sentence of a descriptive paragraph, you should convey a dominant impression about the subject. The dominant impression is the overall impression or feeling that the topic inspires.

topic   controlling idea
When Amory was five, he was already a delightful companion for her.

—F. Scott Fitzgerald, *This Side of Paradise*

topic   controlling idea
Lady Patricia was a perfect example of beauty that is but skin deep.

—Nancy Mitford, *Love in a Cold Climate*

The Writer's Desk Write Topic Sentences

Write a topic sentence for each of the following topics. You can look for ideas in the Warm Up on pages 76–77. Each topic sentence should state what you are describing and contain a controlling idea.

EXAMPLE:

Topic: A useless product

Topic sentence: When I was nine years old, I was desperate to own a Furby.

1. Topic: An emotional moment

   Topic sentence: _____

   _____

2. Topic: Food quirks (unusual food habits or foods you love or hate)

   Topic sentence: _____

   _____

3. Topic: A busy place

   Topic sentence: _____

   _____

The Supporting Ideas

After you have developed an effective topic sentence, generate supporting details. The details can be placed in space, time, or emphatic order.

 **Using Vivid Language**

When you write a descriptive paragraph, try to use **vivid language.** Use specific action verbs and adjectives to create a clear picture of what you are describing.

She looked ~~nice~~. *stunning*   (Use a more vivid, specific adjective.)

The young man ~~left~~ *bolted from* the room.   (Use a more vivid, specific verb.)

PRACTICE 2

Each sentence contains a familiar word in italics. Write down at least two more descriptive ways to say each word. Try to find words that are more specific.

EXAMPLE:

She *laughed* during her gym class.   *giggled, snickered, chuckled*

1. I *ran* to work. _____

2. She *shouted* at her sister. _____

3. She felt *surprised* when she won the award. _____

4. That is a *bad* movie. _____

5. The child was *nice*. _____

List Sensory Details

To create a dominant impression, think about your topic, and make a list of your feelings and impressions. These details can include imagery (images that appeal to sight, sound, hearing, taste, and smell).

TOPIC: An abandoned building

Details: —damp floors
—boarded-up windows
—broken glass
—graffiti on the walls
—musty
—gray bricks
—chipping paint

ESSAY LINK

When you plan a descriptive essay, it is useful to list sensory details.

The Writer's Desk List Sensory Details

Think about images, impressions, and feelings that the following topics inspire in you. Refer to your topic sentences on page 80, and make a list under each topic.

EXAMPLE: A useless product:

Furby looks like a strange bird

black and white fur

round owl-like eyes

pointy beak that opens

a hard plastic body under the fur

speaks in a low, gurgling voice

not cuddly

1. An emotional moment: _____

_____

_____

_____

_____

_____

_____

_____

2. Food quirks: _____

_____

_____

_____

_____

_____

3. A busy place: _____

_____

_____

_____

_____

_____

The Paragraph Plan

A descriptive paragraph should contain specific details so that the reader can clearly imagine what is being described. When you make a paragraph plan, remember to include concrete details. Also think about the organizational method that you will use.

ESSAY LINK

In a descriptive essay, place the thesis statement in the introduction. Then, develop each supporting idea in a body paragraph.

TOPIC SENTENCE:	When I was nine years old, I was desperate to own a Furby.
Support 1:	The toy looks like a small owl.
Details:	—large round eyes —small yellow beak
Support 2:	It learns to speak and repeat words.
Details:	—has a low, gurgling voice —does not say many things

Support 3:   The hard plastic body is not cuddly.
    Details: —cannot bring it to bed
               —sits on a counter
Support 4:   The toy becomes boring quickly.
    Details: —after it says a few words, the novelty wears off
               —cannot really be played with because it is fragile

The Writer's Desk **Write a Paragraph Plan**

Choose one of the topic sentences that you wrote for the Writer's Desk on page 80, and write a detailed paragraph plan. You can include some of the sensory details that you have generated in the previous Writer's Desk on page 82.

Topic sentence: _____

_____

Support 1: _____

   Details: _____

_____

_____

Support 2: _____

   Details: _____

_____

_____

Support 3: _____

   Details: _____

_____

_____

The First Draft

After you outline your ideas in a plan, you are ready to write the first draft. Remember to write complete sentences. You might include transitional words or expressions to help your ideas flow smoothly.

Transitional Words and Expressions

You can use space order to describe a person, place, or thing. The following transitions are useful in descriptive paragraphs.

To Show Place or Position			
above	beyond	in the distance	outside
behind	closer in	nearby	over there
below	farther out	on the left/right	under
beside	in front	on top	underneath

The Writer's Desk   Write the First Draft

In the previous Writer's Desk on page 83, you developed a paragraph plan. Now write the first draft of your descriptive paragraph. Before you write, carefully review your paragraph plan and make any necessary changes.

REVISING AND EDITING

Revise and Edit a Descriptive Paragraph

When you finish writing a descriptive paragraph, carefully review your work and revise it to make the description as clear as possible to your readers. Check that you have organized your steps logically, and remove any irrelevant details.

PRACTICE 3

Read the following student paragraph and answer the questions.

When I was nine years old, I was desperate to own a Furby. In 1998, an onslaught of television commercials announced the product, and a Furby craze developed. I begged my mother for the furry little toy. Even though it was expensive and hard to find. I whined so much that my mother bought me one for my birthday. When I opened the package, I was initialy thrilled. It looked like a small owl, with large round eyes and a yellow pointy beak. Black and white fur covered its hard plastic body. Unfortunately, I could not cuddle it and bring it to bed because it was too fragile. The toy was suppose to speak, but the instructions were complicated. I became disappointed because it only repeated a few words in a low gurgling voice, and the toy quickly became boring. After two weeks, I dropped my Furby, and it stopped speaking, so I never played with it again. I have other toys that I stopped using soon after I bought them. Now the Furby is in a box somewhere in my closet, and I feel ridiculous for having wanted such a useless product.

Revising

1. Underline the topic sentence.

2. What is the dominant impression in this paragraph? Circle the best answer.
   a. Anger   b. Disappointment   c. Joy   d. Tension

3. Highlight three vivid verbs in the paragraph.

4. Revise the paragraph for unity. Cross out a sentence that does not belong.

Editing

5. A fragment lacks a subject or verb and is an incomplete sentence. Identify and correct one fragment in the paragraph.

6. This paragraph contains a misspelled word. Circle it and correct it.

7. This paragraph contains a past participle error. Circle and correct it.

The Writer's Desk Revise and Edit Your Paragraph

Revise and edit the paragraph that you wrote for the previous Writer's Desk. Ensure that your paragraph has unity, adequate support, and coherence. Also correct any errors in grammar, spelling, punctuation, and mechanics.

REFLECT ON IT

Think about what you have learned in this chapter. If you do not know an answer, review that topic.

1. What are the main features of a descriptive paragraph? _____

_____

_____

2. Define imagery. _____

3. Look at the familiar words below. Write down at least two more descriptive ways to say each word. Try to find words that are more specific.

a. Cute _____   b. Angry _____

c. Sad _____   d. Mean _____

The Writer's Room   **Topics for Descriptive Paragraphs**

Writing Activity 1

Choose any of the following topics, or choose your own topic. Then write a descriptive paragraph.

General Topics

1. a coffee shop
2. an interesting house or building
3. a useless product or item
4. an evening out
5. a scene from nature
6. a silly fashion trend

College and Work-Related Topics

1. a quiet area on campus
2. an unusual student or co-worker
3. a loud place
4. appropriate work clothing
5. a difficult job
6. an embarrassing moment at work

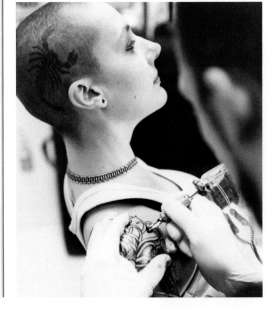

Writing Activity 2

Visit a public place and take notes about the sights, sounds, and smells. Then, write a paragraph describing that place. Include vivid details.

DESCRIPTIVE PARAGRAPH CHECKLIST

As you write your description paragraph, review the checklist on the inside front cover. Also ask yourself the following questions.

☐ Does my topic sentence clearly show what I will describe?

☐ Does my topic sentence have a controlling idea that makes a point about the topic?

☐ Does my paragraph make a dominant impression?

☐ Does my paragraph contain supporting details that appeal to the reader's senses?

☐ Do I use vivid language?

CHAPTER 7

Process

> *It is easier to know how to do something than it is to do it.*
> —CHINESE PROVERB

A pastry chef begins with basic ingredients and follows a process to end up with a delicious dessert. In process writing, you can describe how to do something.

EXPLORING

Explore Topics

In the Warm Up, you will try an exploring strategy to generate ideas about different topics.

The Writer's Desk Warm Up

Think about the following questions, and write down the first ideas that come to your mind. Try to think of two or three ideas for each topic.

EXAMPLE: Imagine that you have a new opportunity and want to leave your current job. What are some things that you should do before you quit your job?

-give supervisor a lot of notice (needs time to hire someone else)

-ask for a reference letter (I might need it later)

-have a going-away party, and thank co-workers and supervisor

1. When you feel stressed, what do you do to relax?

_____

_____

_____

2. What are some things you should do to succeed in college?

_____

_____

_____

3. What are some events, holidays, or ceremonies that require a great deal of preparation?

_____

_____

_____

What Is a Process?

A **process** is a series of steps done in chronological order. In process writing, you explain how to do something, how an incident took place, or how something works.

You explain processes every day. At home, you may explain to a family member how to use an electronic appliance. You may need to give written instructions to a baby-sitter or caregiver. At college, you may explain how to perform a scientific experiment or how a new product was invented. At work, you may explain how to operate a machine or how to do a particular job. The *Process at Work* paragraph on the following page shows how process writing is used in a workplace situation.

The Process Paragraph

There are two main types of process paragraphs.

■ **Complete a process.** This type of paragraph contains directions on how to complete a particular task. For example, a writer might explain how to paint a picture, how to repair a leaky faucet, or how to get a job. The reader should be able to follow the directions and complete the task.

■ **Understand a process.** This type of paragraph explains how something works or how something happens. In other words, the goal is to help the reader understand a process rather than do a process. For example, a writer might explain how the heart pumps blood to other organs in the body or how a country elects its political leaders.

ESSAY LINK

Process essays also focus on completing or understanding a process.

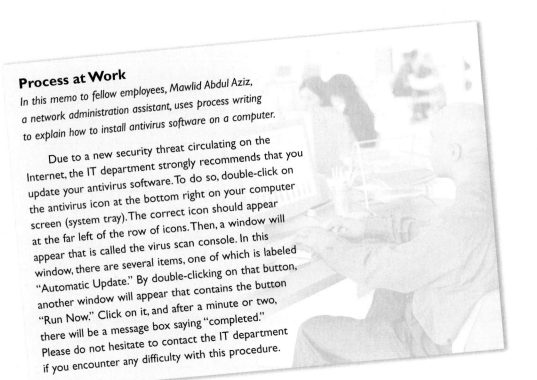

Process at Work

In this memo to fellow employees, Mawlid Abdul Aziz, a network administration assistant, uses process writing to explain how to install antivirus software on a computer.

Due to a new security threat circulating on the Internet, the IT department strongly recommends that you update your antivirus software. To do so, double-click on the antivirus icon at the bottom right on your computer screen (system tray). The correct icon should appear at the far left of the row of icons. Then, a window will appear that is called the virus scan console. In this window, there are several items, one of which is labeled "Automatic Update." By double-clicking on that button, another window will appear that contains the button "Run Now." Click on it, and after a minute or two, there will be a message box saying "completed." Please do not hesitate to contact the IT department if you encounter any difficulty with this procedure.

PRACTICE I

Read the next paragraph and answer the questions.

Packing for a move does not have to be stressful. Moving is already stressful enough. If you are going to pack up your house, however, you might as well do it properly. Do not spend time and money transporting junk. Take a deep breath and go through it all. Have a garage sale, or give junk to organizations that can put your unwanted items to good use. Now, set aside space for packing, and, if you can, **designate** a table or workbench so you can pack at a comfortable height. "You will also want," says Dan Descheneau of Two Small Men With Big Hearts Moving, "a portable packing kit with marking pens, tape measure, tape, twine, and scissors. Carry it with you around the home as you pack." Other things you will need are boxes, bubble wrap, or newsprint. The best way to pack is room by room. Pack from least to most important items. Begin with seasonal clothing, sports equipment, etc. Things you will need first and during the move should be packed last. This includes telephones, address books, bills, clothes, toiletries, medicine, maps, food, and drink.

—Joel Ceausu, "How to Pack Up a House," *Montreal Gazette*

designate: to choose

1. a. What is the topic of this paragraph? _____

   _____

   b. What is the controlling idea in the topic sentence? _____

   _____

2. What type of process paragraph is this? Circle the best answer.

   a. Complete a process.   b. Understand a process.

3. Look at the paragraph and number each step. What are the main steps that you should take when you move? List each step.

    _____

    _____

    _____

    _____

    _____

4. This paragraph does not have a concluding sentence. Write a concluding sentence that sums up the main ideas in this paragraph.

    _____

    _____

PRACTICE 2

Scrabble, one of the world's most popular board games, has an interesting history. Read the next paragraph and answer the questions.

Alfred Mosher Butts, a quiet architect from Poughkeepsie, New York, was unemployed when he invented the world's most popular word game. Lexico was played without a board, and players earned points based on the lengths of words that they could build. By carefully analyzing the *New York Times*, Butts discovered that *S* is the most frequently used letter, so he reduced the number of *S*'s in the game, and he gave additional points to letters such as *J*, *Q*, and *Z*. Unable to interest game companies, Butts produced the games himself and sold them to friends. Then in 1938, inspired by crossword puzzles, Butts combined the letters with a playing board and renamed his game Criss-Cross, but game manufacturers continued to reject his idea. Things finally changed for Butts in 1948, when a small entrepreneur, James Brunot, picked up Butts's game and renamed it Scrabble. By 1953, the demand for Scrabble was so great that a large manufacturer licensed and mass-produced the game. According to Mattel Incorporated, Scrabble is now the world's best-selling board game, with over 100 million copies sold in 29 different languages.

—Iannick Di Sanza, student

1. Underline the topic sentence of this paragraph.

2. What type of process paragraph is this? Circle the best answer.
   a. Complete a process   b. Understand a process

3. Look at the paragraph and number the steps that Alfred Butts took to complete his board game.

PRACTICE 3

For each of the following topics, write *C* if it explains how to complete a process, or write *U* if it explains how to understand a process (how something works or how something happens).

1. How to discipline a child   _____

2. The stages in a child's development   _____

3. How a cell phone works   _____

4. Things to remember when you write a song   _____

5. Five ways to keep your motorcycle in top condition _____

6. The chemical process of a firefly's light   _____

DEVELOPING

ESSAY LINK

In a process essay, the thesis statement expresses the controlling idea.

When you write a process paragraph, choose a process that you can easily cover in a single paragraph. For example, you might be able to explain how to send an e-mail message in a single paragraph; however, you would need much more than a paragraph to explain how to use a particular computer software program.

The Topic Sentence

In a process paragraph, the topic sentence states what process you will be explaining and what readers will be able to do or understand after they have read the paragraph.

topic   controlling idea

To calm your child during a tantrum, <u>follow the next steps</u>.

controlling idea   topic

<u>With inexpensive materials,</u> **you can redecorate a room in your house.**

> ⟨ **Hint** ⟩   **Make a Point**
>
> Your topic sentence should not simply announce the topic. It should make a point about the topic.
>
> **Announces:**   This is how you do speed dating.
>
>   controlling idea   topic
>
> **Correct:**   <u>It is surprisingly easy and efficient</u> **to meet someone using speed dating.**

The Writer's Desk **Write Topic Sentences**

Write a topic sentence for each of the following topics. You can look for ideas in the Warm Up on pages 88–89. Each topic sentence should state the process and should contain a controlling idea.

EXAMPLE:

Topic: How to leave a job

Topic sentence: _If you want to leave your job on a positive note, there are a few things that you should consider._

1. Topic: How to relax

   Topic sentence: _____

   _____

2. Topic: How to succeed in college

   Topic sentence: _____

   _____

3. Topic: How to prepare for a specific event

   Topic sentence: _____

   _____

The Supporting Ideas

A process paragraph contains a series of steps. When you develop supporting ideas for a process paragraph, think about the main steps that are necessary to complete the process. Most process paragraphs use time order.

> **ESSAY LINK**
>
> In an essay, each body paragraph could describe a process. For example, in an essay about how to get rich, one body paragraph could be about buying lottery tickets and another could be about inventing a product.

Hint **Give Steps, Not Examples**

When you explain how to complete a process, describe each step. Do not simply list examples of the process.

Topic: How to Get Rich

List of Examples	Steps in the Process
- write a bestseller	- do market research
- win the lottery	- find a specific need
- invent a product	- invent a product to fulfill that need
- inherit money	- heavily promote the product

The Writer's Desk **List Main Steps**

Think about three or four essential steps for each process. Make a list under each topic.

EXAMPLE: How to leave a job

explain your reason for going

give enough notice

ask for a reference letter

find out about benefits

2. How to succeed in college

_____

_____

_____

_____

1. How to relax

_____

_____

_____

_____

3. How to prepare for an event

_____

_____

_____

_____

ESSAY LINK

In a process essay, place the thesis statement in the introduction. Then use each body paragraph to explain a step in the process.

The Paragraph Plan

A paragraph plan helps you organize your topic sentence and supporting details before writing a first draft. Decide which steps and which details your reader will really need to complete the process or understand it. Write down the steps in chronological order.

TOPIC SENTENCE:	If you want to leave your job on a positive note, there are a few things that you should consider.
Step 1:	Give positive reasons for leaving.
Details:	—do not complain about the company —say you need a new challenge
Step 2:	Give employers enough notice.
Details:	—the company might need time to hire a replacement
Step 3:	Ask for a reference letter.
Details:	—may need it in the future
Step 4:	Find out about employment benefits.
Details:	—might get unused vacation pay

Hint **Include Necessary Tools or Supplies**

When you are writing a plan for a process paragraph, remember to include any special tools or supplies a reader will need to complete the process. For example, if you want to explain how to pack for a move, you should mention that you need boxes, felt-tip markers, newsprint, twine, scissors, and tape.

The Writer's Desk **Write a Paragraph Plan**

Choose one of the topic sentences that you wrote for the Writer's Desk on page 93, and then list the main steps to complete the process. Also add details and examples that will help to explain each step.

Topic sentence: _____

_____

Supporting points:

Step 1: _____

  Details: _____

_____

Step 2: _____

  Details: _____

_____

Step 3: _____

  Details: _____

_____

Step 4: _____

  Details: _____

_____

Step 5: _____

  Details: _____

_____

The First Draft

After you outline your ideas in a plan, you are ready to write the first draft. Remember to write complete sentences. You might include transitional words or expressions to help your ideas flow smoothly.

 **Using Commands**

In process writing, address the reader directly. For example, instead of writing "You should travel in a group," you could simply write "Travel in a group."

Transitional Words and Expressions

Most process paragraphs explain a process using time (or chronological) order. The following transitions are useful in process paragraphs.

To Begin a Process	To Continue a Process		To End a Process
(at) first	after that	later	eventually
initially	afterward	meanwhile	finally
the first step	also	second	in the end
	furthermore	then	ultimately
	in addition	third	

The Writer's Desk   **Write the First Draft**

In the previous Writer's Desk on page 95, you developed a paragraph plan. Now write the first draft of your process paragraph. Before you write, carefully review your paragraph plan and make any necessary changes.

REVISING AND EDITING

Revise and Edit a Process Paragraph

When you finish writing a process paragraph, carefully review your work and revise it to make the process as clear as possible to your readers. Check to make sure that you have organized your steps chronologically and remove any irrelevant details.

PRACTICE 4

Read the next student paragraph and answer the questions.

If you want to leave your job on a positive note, there are a few things that you should consider. First, give a positive reason for leaving. Instead of complaining about something in the company, you could say that you need a change and want a different challenge. Give as much notice as possible, this will leave a favorable impression. It will also give your boss time to find a replacement. If you think you deserve it, ask for a reference letter. Even if you already have a new job, the reference letter could be useful at a future date. Find out if you are entitled to benefits. You may be eligible for back pay or vacation pay. Business consultant Cho Matsu says "The impression you make when you leave a job could have an impact on your future career".

Revising

1. Underline the topic sentence.

2. The author uses *first* to introduce the first step. Subsequent steps would be more clearly recognizable if the writer had used more transitions. Indicate, with a number, where more transitional expressions could be added, and write possible examples on the lines provided.

   _____

   _____

   _____

3. How does the writer conclude the paragraph?
   a. With a prediction   b. With a suggestion   c. With a quotation

Editing

4. This paragraph contains a type of run-on sentence called a comma splice. Two complete sentences are incorrectly connected with a comma. Identify and correct the comma splice.

5. This paragraph contains two punctuation errors in the direct quotation. Correct the mistakes directly on the paragraph.

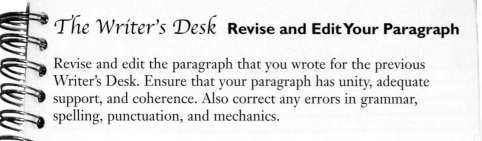

The Writer's Desk   Revise and Edit Your Paragraph

Revise and edit the paragraph that you wrote for the previous Writer's Desk. Ensure that your paragraph has unity, adequate support, and coherence. Also correct any errors in grammar, spelling, punctuation, and mechanics.

REFLECT ON IT

Think about what you have learned in this unit. If you do not know an answer, review that topic.

1. What are the two types of process paragraphs? Briefly explain each type.

   a. _____

   _____

   b. _____

   _____

2. What organizational method is generally used in process writing? Circle the best answer.

   a. Space order   b. Time order   c. Emphatic order

3. Why are transitional words important in process writing?

   _____

   _____

The Writer's Room   **Topics for Process Paragraphs**

Writing Activity 1

Choose any of the following topics, or choose your own topic. Then write a process paragraph.

General Topics

1. how to make your home safe
2. how to decorate a room with very little money
3. how to make a friend
4. how to break up with a mate
5. how to train a pet
6. how to build something

College and Work-Related Topics

7. how to choose a college
8. how to stay motivated at college
9. how to prepare for a job interview
10. how to get along with your co-workers
11. how to organize your desk or tools
12. how something was discovered

Writing Activity 2

Pop artist Andy Warhol once said that everyone would be famous for fifteen minutes. Think of some processes related to fame. Some ideas might be how to become famous, how to stay famous, how to lose fame, how to survive fame, or how to meet a celebrity. Then, write a process paragraph.

PROCESS PARAGRAPH CHECKLIST

As you write your process paragraph, review the checklist on the inside front cover. Also ask yourself the following questions.

Does my topic sentence make a point about the process?

Do I include all of the steps in the process?

Do I clearly explain each step so my reader can accomplish the process or understand it?

Do I mention all of the supplies that my reader needs to complete the process?

Do I use transitions to connect all of the steps in the process?

CHAPTER 8

Definition

" A successful marriage requires falling in love many times, always with the same person. "

—MIGNON MCLAUGHLIN
American journalist (1913–1983)

CONTENTS

For many people, the definition of happiness is having a loving relationship with someone. In definition writing, you define what a term means.

EXPLORING

Explore Topics

In the Warm Up, you will try an exploring strategy to generate ideas about different topics.

The Writer's Desk **Warm Up**

Think about the following questions, and write down the first ideas that come to your mind. Try to think of two or three ideas for each topic.

EXAMPLE: What is an optimist? Think of some qualities that an optimist has.

Always sees the bright side of life

Doesn't dwell on bad things and hopes for the best

Is usually pretty happy, which can be annoying

1. What are some qualities that a leader should have?

_____

_____

_____

2. What is talent? Give examples of talent.

_____

_____

_____

3. What are some characteristics of a workaholic?

_____

_____

_____

What Is Definition?

When you **define,** you explain the meaning of a word. Some terms have concrete meanings, and you can define them in a few words. For example, a pebble is "a small stone." Other words, such as *culture, happiness,* or *evil,* are more abstract and require longer definitions. In fact, it is possible to write a paragraph, an essay, or even an entire book on such concepts.

The simplest way to define a term is to look it up in a dictionary. However, many words have nuances that are not necessarily discussed in dictionaries. For example, suppose that your boss calls your work "unsatisfactory." You might need clarification of that term. Do you have poor work habits? Do you miss deadlines? Is your attitude problematic? What does your boss mean by "unsatisfactory?"

The ability to define difficult concepts is always useful. At home, a friend or loved one may ask you to define *commitment.* If you mention that a movie was *great,* you may need to clarify what you mean by that word. In a political science class, you might define *socialism, capitalism,* or *communism.* At work, you might define your company's *winning strategy.* The *Definition at Work* paragraph on the following page shows definition writing used in a workplace situation.

The Definition Paragraph

When you write a definition paragraph, try to explain what a term means to you. For example, if someone asks you to define *bravery,* you might tell stories to illustrate the meaning of the word. You may also give examples of acts of bravery. You might even explain what bravery is not.

When you write a definition paragraph, remember the following two points.

■ **Choose a term that you know something about.** You need to understand a term in order to say something relevant and interesting about it.

■ **Give a clear definition.** In your first sentence, write a definition that is understandable to your reader, and support your definition with examples.

Hint **Consider Your Audience**

When you write a definition paragraph, consider your audience. You may have to adjust your tone and vocabulary, depending on who reads the paragraph. For example, if you write a definition paragraph about computer viruses for your English class, you will have to use easily understandable terms. If you write the same paragraph for your computer class, you can use more technical terms.

Definition at Work

In the following memo to a parent, reading specialist Amanda Wong defines a common reading disorder.

As we have discussed, your daughter exhibits signs of a reading disorder commonly referred to as dyslexia. Dyslexia is not the result of damage to the brain or nervous system. It is, more accurately, a problem that is often found in visual learners. Such learners associate pictures with words. For example, your daughter would associate the word *tiger* with the animal, but she has no image to associate with words such as *a* or *the*. Therefore, she may become confused when she reads such words. A feeling of disorientation when reading the letters in words can further compound the problem. She may not perceive individual letters in sequence but might interpret them in a variety of orders and directions. Thus, a dyslexic child may see the word *dog* as *god* or *bog*. In our next meeting, I will give you some strategies to help your daughter with her reading.

PRACTICE 1

Read the paragraph, and then answer the questions.

innate: built in

"Cool" can be described as a certain **innate** quality that clearly sets something above its surroundings and makes one wish to be associated with it. There must be a certain degree of exclusivity associated with cool things; they should make you feel like you're superior to the general public. Cool things often involve expending some effort to associate with them. For example, the popular 1990s sitcom *Seinfeld* was indisputably an excellent show, but it was not cool because everybody watched it. On the other hand, it was cool to watch *Seinfeld* during its first two seasons when nobody had heard of it, and when it changed time slots every other week. It should be noted that, occasionally, something's coolness is so entrenched that it overcomes the popularity factor and remains on the list. These occasions are rare, however, and usually only apply to the most elite. For example, the Beatles disbanded in 1970, yet a lot of people would say the band is still cool.

—Paul Sabourin, "What Is Cool"

1. Underline the topic sentence.

2. What is the writer defining? _____

_____

3. List the supporting details. _____

_____

_____

_____

4. Think of another example to add to this paragraph. _____

_____

DEVELOPING

The Topic Sentence

A clear topic sentence for a definition paragraph introduces the term and provides a definition. There are three basic ways to define a term.

- By synonym
- By category
- By negation

ESSAY LINK

In a definition essay, the thesis statement expresses the controlling idea. In the thesis, you can define the term by synonym, category, or negation.

Definition by Synonym

The easiest way to define a term is to supply a synonym (a word that has a similar meaning). This type of definition is useful if the original term is difficult to understand and the synonym is a more familiar word.

term	+	synonym
A Mickey Mouse course		is an easy course to complete.
I am a procrastinator,		which means I tend to put things off.

Definition by Category

A more effective way to define a term is to give a definition by category (or class). When you define by category, you determine the larger group to which the term belongs. Then you determine what unique characteristics set the term apart from others in that category.

	term	+	category	+	detail

A kingfisher is   a type of bird   that is small and brightly colored.

Luddites   are people   who are skeptical about new technology.

Definition by Negation

When you define by negation, you explain what a term does not mean. You can then include a sentence explaining what it does mean.

     term   +   what it is not   +   what it is

Alcoholism   is not an invented disease;   it is a serious physical dependency.

Hackers   are not playful computer geeks;   they are criminals.

PRACTICE 2

A. Write a one-sentence definition by synonym for each of the following terms. Your definition should include the term and a synonym. If necessary, you can look up the terms in the dictionary; however, define each one using your own words.

EXAMPLE:

To capitulate <u>means to give up or surrender.</u>

1. Ravenous _____

2. A celebrity _____

3. Malaria _____

B. Write a one-sentence definition by category for the following terms. Make sure that your definition includes the term, a category, and details.

EXAMPLE:

A cockroach <u>is an insect that lives in the cracks and crevices of</u>
             <u>buildings.</u>

4. Stilettos _____

   _____

5. Paparazzi _____

   _____

6. A deadbeat parent _____

   _____

C. Write a one-sentence definition by negation for the following terms. Explain what each term is not, followed by what each term is.

EXAMPLE:

A television addict *is not a regular TV viewer but a person who*
watches television excessively.

7. A placebo _____

_____

8. Good parents _____

_____

9. A dog _____

_____

> ## Hint   **Be Precise!**
>
> When you write a definition paragraph, it is important to use the precise words to define the term. Moreover, when you define a term by category, make sure that the category for your term is correct. For example, look at the following imprecise definitions of insomnia.
>
> Insomnia is the (inability) to sleep well.
> (Insomnia is not an ability or an inability.)
> Insomnia is (when) you cannot sleep well.
> (*When* refers to a time, but insomnia is not a time.)
> Insomnia is the (nights) when you do not get enough sleep.
> (Insomnia is not days or nights.)
> Insomnia is (where) it is hard to fall asleep.
> (*Where* refers to a place, but insomnia is not a place.)
>
> Now look at a better definition of insomnia.
>
>   category
> Insomnia is a **sleeping disorder** characterized by the inability to sleep well.

PRACTICE 3

Revise each sentence using precise language.

EXAMPLE:

Tuning out is when you ignore something.

Tuning out is the action of ignoring something.

1. A scapegoat is when a person gets blamed for something.

_____

2. Claustrophobia is the inability to be in a small place.

_____

3. A bully is the abuse of power over others.

   _____

   _____

4. Adolescence is where you are between childhood and adulthood.

   _____

   _____

5. Ego surfing is when you surf the Internet to find references to yourself.

   _____

   _____

The Writer's Desk Write Topic Sentences

Write a topic sentence in which you define each of the following topics. You can look for ideas in the Warm Up on pages 100–101. Remember to use precise language in your definition.

EXAMPLE:

Topic: An optimist

Topic sentence: *An optimist is a person who always looks on the bright side of life.*

1. Topic: A leader

   Topic sentence: _____

   _____

2. Topic: Talent

   Topic sentence: _____

   _____

3. Topic: A workaholic

   Topic sentence: _____

   _____

The Supporting Ideas

After you have developed an effective topic sentence, generate supporting ideas. In a definition paragraph, you can give examples that clarify your definition.

Think about how you will organize your examples. Most definition paragraphs use emphatic order, which means that examples are placed from the most to the least important or from the least to the most important.

The Writer's Desk **Develop Supporting Ideas**

Choose one of your topic sentences from the Writer's Desk on page 106. List three or four examples that best illustrate the definition.

EXAMPLE: An optimist is a person who always looks at the bright side of life.

> sees things positively
> is healthy
> genetic?
> has a longer life span

Topic sentence: _____

_____

Supports: _____

_____

_____

_____

The Paragraph Plan

A good definition paragraph includes a complete definition of the term and provides adequate examples to support the central definition. When creating a definition paragraph plan, make sure that your examples provide varied evidence, and do not just repeat the definition. Also add details that will help clarify your supporting examples.

ESSAY LINK

In a definition essay, the thesis statement is in the introduction. Each supporting idea is in a distinct body paragraph with its own topic sentence.

TOPIC SENTENCE:	An optimist is a person who always looks on the bright side of life.
Support 1:	He or she sees positive ways out of negative situations.
Details:	—my mother saw her divorce as a new beginning —contrast to father who saw divorce as a terrible ending
Support 2:	An optimist has a healthy mind and body.
Details:	—tend to be healthier, according to psychiatrists —have lower blood pressure
Support 3:	Optimism runs in families.
Details:	—optimistic parents have optimist children (genetic) —parents model positive attitudes to their children

The Writer's Desk **Write a Paragraph Plan**

Create a detailed paragraph plan using one of the topic sentences that you wrote for the Writer's Desk on page 106. Arrange the supporting details in a logical order.

Topic sentence: _____

_____

Support 1: _____

Details: _____

_____

_____

Support 2: _____

Details: _____

_____

_____

Support 3: _____

Details: _____

_____

_____

The First Draft

After you outline your ideas in a plan, you are ready to write the first draft. Remember to write complete sentences. You might include transitional words or expressions to help your ideas flow smoothly.

Transitional Words and Expressions

Transitional expressions can show different levels of importance. The following transitions are useful in definition paragraphs.

To Show the Level of Importance	
clearly	next
first	one quality . . . another quality
most of all	second
most important	undoubtedly

The Writer's Desk **Write the First Draft**

In the previous Writer's Desk, you developed a paragraph plan. Now write the first draft of your definition paragraph. Before you write, carefully review your paragraph plan and make any necessary changes.

REVISING AND EDITING

Revise and Edit a Definition Paragraph

When you finish writing a definition paragraph, carefully review your work and revise it to make the definition as clear as possible to your readers. Check that you have organized your steps logically, and remove any irrelevant details.

PRACTICE 4

Read the next student paragraph and answer the questions.

> An optimist is a person who always looks on the bright side of life. Optimists see positive ways out of negative situations. They see bad events as temporary and controllable. For example, my mother is an optimist. She divorced my father. She saw the divorce as a new beginning. Now she is very happy. My father, on the contrary, is not an optimist. He saw the divorce as a terrible ending. He stayed depressed. According to an August 2002 study in the *Mayo Clinic Proceedings*, optimists have a more lower risk of premature death. They live longer. People may have a genetic predisposition to optimism. It often run's in families. For example, my grandmother, my mother, and I are all optimists.

Revising

1. Underline the topic sentence.

2. What type of definition does the topic sentence contain? Circle the best answer.
   a. Definition by synonym   b. Definition by category
   c. Definition by negation

3. This paragraph lacks sentence variety. Revise the paragraph to give it more sentence variety by combining sentences or changing the first word of some sentences. (For more information about combining sentences and sentence variety, see Chapters 17–19.)

Editing

4. There is one incorrectly written comparison. Circle the error and correct it.

5. There is one apostrophe error. Circle the error and correct it.

The Writer's Desk Revise and Edit Your Paragraph

Revise and edit the paragraph that you wrote for the previous Writer's Desk.

Ensure that your paragraph has unity, adequate support, and coherence. Also correct any errors in grammar, spelling, punctuation, and mechanics.

REFLECT ON IT

Think about what you have learned in this chapter. If you do not know an answer, review that topic.

1. In definition writing, you _____

   _____

2. Explain each of the following types of definitions. Then give an example of each definition. Use your own ideas.

   a. Explain definition by synonym. _____

   _____

   Give an example of a definition by synonym. _____

   _____

   b. Explain definition by category. _____

   _____

   Give an example of a definition by category. _____

   _____

   c. Explain definition by negation. _____

   _____

   Give an example of a definition by negation. _____

   _____

The Writer's Room

Topics for Definition Paragraphs

Writing Activity 1

Choose any of the following topics, or choose your own topic. Then write a definition paragraph.

General Topics

1. a miracle
2. fame
3. a spoiled child
4. fashion police
5. bling bling
6. mind games

College and Work-Related Topics

7. integrity
8. a slacker
9. a headhunter
10. an opportunist
11. the glass ceiling
12. an apprentice

Writing Activity 2

Write a paragraph in which you define censorship. What sorts of things get censored? Think of some interesting examples that support your definition.

DEFINITION PARAGRAPH CHECKLIST

As you write your definition paragraph, review the checklist on the inside front cover. Also ask yourself the following questions.

- Does my topic sentence contain a definition by synonym, negation, or category?

- Do all of my supporting sentences relate to the topic sentence?

- Do I use concise language in my definition?

- Do I include enough examples to help define the term?

Classification

> *Inanimate objects are classified scientifically into three major categories: those that don't work, those that break down, and those that get lost.*
>
> —RUSSELL BAKER
> *American journalist (b. 1925)*

CONTENTS

In a car lot, cars are classified according to their models and makes. In classification writing, you divide a topic into categories to explain it.

EXPLORING

Explore Topics

In the Warm Up, you will try an exploring strategy to generate ideas about different topics.

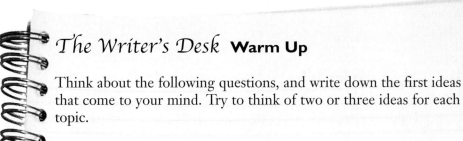

The Writer's Desk Warm Up

Think about the following questions, and write down the first ideas that come to your mind. Try to think of two or three ideas for each topic.

EXAMPLE: What are some different types of diets?

Some people don't eat at all. Starvation diets?

Fad diets. Some diet books become bestsellers.

Protein shakes. Aren't there diet pills?

1. List some clothing that you own. You might think about old clothing, comfortable clothing, beautiful clothing, and so on.

_____

_____

_____

2. What are some different types of consumers? To get ideas, you might think about some people you know and the way that they shop.

_____

_____

_____

3. What are some types of jobs that students can get?

_____

_____

_____

What Is Classification?

When you classify, you sort a subject into more understandable categories. Each of the categories must be part of a larger group, yet they must also be distinct. For example, you might write a paragraph about the most common types of pets and sort the subject into cats, dogs, and birds.

Classification occurs in many situations. At home, you could classify the responsibilities of each person in the family, or you could classify your bills. In a biology course, you might write a paper about the different types of cells, or in a commerce course, you may write about the categories in a financial statement. On the job, you might advertise the different types of products or services that your company sells.

ESSAY LINK

Classification essays also require a classification principle and distinct categories.

The Classification Paragraph

To find a topic for a classification paragraph, think of something that can be sorted into different groups. Also determine a reason for classifying the items. When you are planning your ideas for a classification paragraph, remember these two points.

1. **Use a common classification principle. A classification principle** is the overall method that you use to sort the subject into categories. To find the classification principle, think about one common characteristic that unites the different categories. For example, if your subject is "the telephone," your classification principle might be any of the following:

    – types of annoying phone calls

    – reasons that people buy cell phones

    – types of long-distance services

    – types of customer reactions to telephone salespeople

2. **Sort the subject into distinct categories.** A classification paragraph should have two or more categories.

Topic: Phone calls

Classification principle: Calls that are annoying

Category 1	**Category 2**	**Category 3**
Telephone surveys	Prank calls	Wrong numbers

The following *Classification at Work* paragraph discusses a topic that has been divided into categories.

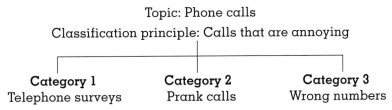

Classification at Work

Robert Luzynski, an allergy specialist, wrote the following information in a brochure for his patients.

If you exhibit allergic symptoms to animals, there are three types of treatment that you can follow. The most effective is to avoid contact with known allergens. Thus, avoid bringing pets into the home. If you have a pet, consider using an air cleaner, vacuum two to three times a week, and ensure that the animal is groomed frequently to remove loose fur and dander. The second type of treatment consists of medications. Antihistamines help alleviate the symptoms of allergic reactions, but they do not cure allergies. It is important to read the labels carefully as some antihistamines cause drowsiness. A final method, desensitization, is an extended treatment involving allergy shots. You would be exposed to gradually increasing amounts of specific allergens. The treatment lasts for an extended period of time, and the goal is to reduce your sensitivity to the allergens.

PRACTICE 1

Read the next paragraph and answer the questions.

Hackers come in three stripes, according to Drew Williams, a computer security specialist for Maryland-based Axent Technologies.

depredations: acts of destruction

There are the "newbies," or inexperienced hackers, who generally stumble upon a Web site offering free hacking software. They try to break into targets through their Web sites as an after-school hobby. "White hat" hackers are more talented—and serious—but they use their talents to expose weak security. According to Williams, "They hack for a cause." White hat infiltrators might squirm into the computer innards of a bank or government ministry and steal a few nuggets of data, but the white hat hacker will then expose his deed to his victim and offer security suggestions—often for a fee. Then there are the "black hat" hackers whose **depredations** include sabotage of government Web sites; the Pentagon and Department of Justice are among favorite targets. They plunder bank deposits, shut down public services such as telephones and electricity, and steal trade secrets, Williams said.

—Kim Krane, "Computer Crime Tops $100 Million," *APBnews.com*

1. Underline the topic sentence of this paragraph.

2. State the three categories that the author discusses and list some details about each category.

   a. _____

      Details: _____

   b. _____

      Details: _____

   c. _____

      Details: _____

3. Who is the audience for this paragraph?

   _____

4. What is the purpose of this paragraph? Circle the best answer.

   a. To persuade   b. To inform   c. To entertain

Making a Classification Chart

A **classification chart** is a visual representation of the main topic and its categories. Making a classification chart can help you identify the categories more clearly so that you will be able to write more exact topic sentences.

When you classify items, remember to use a single method of classification and a common classification principle to sort the items. For example, if you are classifying movies, you might classify them according to their ratings: General Audience, Parental Guidance, and Restricted. You could also classify movies according to their country of origin: British, American, and French, for example. Remember that one classification principle must unite the group.

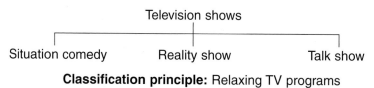

Television shows

Situation comedy   Reality show   Talk show

Classification principle: Relaxing TV programs

> **Hint**   **Categories Should Not Overlap**
>
> When sorting a topic into categories, make sure that the categories do not overlap. For example, you would not classify drivers into careful drivers, aggressive drivers, and bad drivers, because aggressive drivers could also be bad drivers. Each category should be distinct.

PRACTICE 2

In the following classification charts, a subject has been broken down into distinct categories. The items in the group should have the same classification principle. Cross out one item in each group that does not belong. Then write down the classification principle that unites the group.

EXAMPLE:

Cars

| Japan | U.S. | Germany | ~~economy~~ |

Classification principle: *Car-producing countries*

1.

Dogs

| Miniature poodle | Great Dane | Doberman | Saint Bernard |

Classification principle: _____

2.

Food

| Soda pop | Hamburgers | French fries | Fresh fruit |

Classification principle: _____

3.

Books

| Paperback | Hardcover | Best-sellers | Online |

Classification principle: _____

4.

Sports

| Cycling | Rock climbing | Bungee jumping | Skydiving |

Classification principle: _____

5.

Items in my home

| Nice photograph | Broken chair | Clothing that does not fit | Book I'll never read |

Classification principle: _____

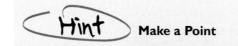

Make a Point

To make interesting classification paragraphs, try to express an attitude, opinion, or feeling about the topic. For example, you can write a paragraph about types of diets, but it is more interesting if you make a point about the types of diets.

Poor:	Types of diets
Better:	Types of **dangerous** diets
	Types of **effective** diets

The Writer's Desk **Find Distinct Categories**

Break down the following topics into three distinct categories. Remember to find categories that do not overlap. You can look for ideas in the Warm Up on page 113.

EXAMPLE: Diets

Crash diets   Liquid diets   Magic-pill diets

Classification principle: Types of dangerous diets

1.   Clothing

_____   _____   _____

Classification principle: _____

2.   Consumers

_____   _____   _____

Classification principle: _____

3.   Student jobs

_____   _____   _____

Classification principle: _____

DEVELOPING

The Topic Sentence

The topic sentence in a classification paragraph clearly indicates what a writer will classify. It also includes the controlling idea, which is the classification principle that you use.

ESSAY LINK

In a classification essay, the thesis statement expresses the controlling idea or classification principle.

Several types of students can completely disrupt a classroom.

Topic:	Students
Classification principle:	Disruptive types

You can also mention the types of categories in your topic sentence.

The most annoying telephone calls are surveys, prank calls, and wrong numbers.

Topic:	Telephone calls
Classification principle:	Types of annoying calls

The Writer's Desk **Write Topic Sentences**

Look again at what you wrote in the Warm Up on page 113. Also look at the classification charts that you made for each topic. Now write clear topic sentences. Remember that your topic sentence can include the different categories you will be discussing.

EXAMPLE: Diets

Dieters sometimes use dangerous methods to lose weight, such as the high-fat diet, the liquid diet, and the magic-pill diet.

1. Topic: Clothing

   Topic sentence: _____

   _____

2. Topic: Consumers

   Topic sentence: _____

   _____

3. Topic: Student jobs

   Topic sentence: _____

   _____

ESSAY LINK

You can make a detailed classification chart when you develop your classification essay. Each supporting idea would become a distinct paragraph.

The Supporting Ideas

After you have developed an effective topic sentence, generate supporting ideas. In a classification paragraph, you can list details about each of your categories.

The Paragraph Plan

You can make a standard paragraph plan. Another way to visualize your categories and your supporting ideas is to make a detailed classification chart. Break down the main topic into several categories, and then give details about each category.

Dieters sometimes use dangerous methods to lose weight, such as the high-fat diet, the liquid diet, and the magic pill diet.

High-fat diets	Liquid diets	Magic-pill diets
- point is to completely cut out carbohydrates - focus on animal and vegetable fats and oils - may cause heart disease	- drink only liquids for many days - milkshake diet - water diet - fruit juice diet - dangerous malnutrition	- pills reduce calories - fat-burning pills - appetite reduction pills - caffeine diet pills - herbal diet pills - deaths associated with pill diets

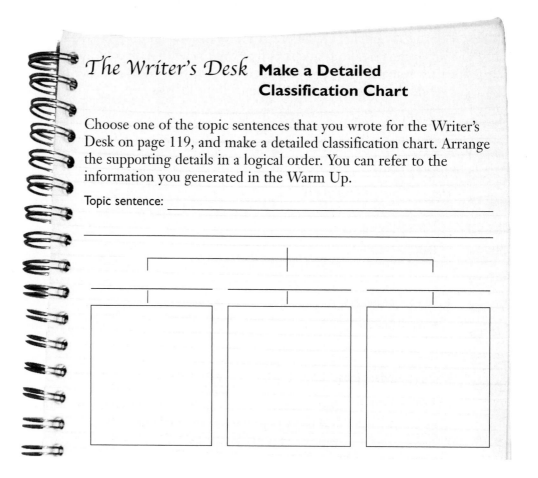

The Writer's Desk Make a Detailed Classification Chart

Choose one of the topic sentences that you wrote for the Writer's Desk on page 119, and make a detailed classification chart. Arrange the supporting details in a logical order. You can refer to the information you generated in the Warm Up.

Topic sentence: _____

_____

 **Use the Chart as a Plan**

Your classification chart can also serve as your paragraph plan. Like a paragraph plan, your chart contains your topic sentence, your categories, and details about each category.

The First Draft

After you outline your ideas in a classification chart or plan, you are ready to write the first draft. Remember to write complete sentences. You might include transitional words or expressions to help your ideas flow smoothly.

Transitional Words and Expressions

Some classification paragraphs use transitional words and expressions to show which category is most important and to signal a movement from one category to the next. The next transitions are very useful in classification writing.

To Show Importance	To Show Types of Categories
above all	one kind ... another kind
clearly	the first/second type
the most important	the first/second kind
most of all	the last category
particularly	

The Writer's Desk **Write the First Draft**

Write the first draft of your classification paragraph. Before you write, carefully review your detailed classification chart and make any necessary changes.

REVISING AND EDITING

Revise and Edit a Classification Paragraph

When you finish writing a classification paragraph, carefully review your work and revise it to make sure that the categories do not overlap. Check to make sure that you have organized your paragraph logically, and remove any irrelevant details.

PRACTICE 3

Read the next student paragraph and answer the questions.

Dieters sometimes use dangerous methods to lose weight, such as high-fat diets, liquid diets, fad diets, and the magic pill diets. With high-fat diets, the point is to cut out carbohydrates. The dieter can eat as much animal protein and fat as he or she likes. However, this diet can cause high cholesterol. Another dangerous weight-loss method is the liquid diet. People have liquid meals, but if they continue this diet for a long time, they can become malnourished. One more common type of diet is the fad diet. Somebody promotes a new, improved weight-loss method, and people blindly follow this latest diet fad. For example, in the Atkins diet, dieters limit their intake of carbohydrates, or in the liquid protein diet, you just drink a protein beverage. The last type of diet, magic pills. People rely on pills such as caffeine or appetite-reduction pills to lose weight. The fen-phen diet was very popular for a while, but the pills sometimes had fatal side effects.

Revising

1. What is the classification principle in this paragraph? _____

2. What are the four categories? _____

   _____

3. Which category is not valid? _____

   Explain why. _____

   _____

4. This paragraph does not have a concluding sentence. Write a concluding sentence in the space. The concluding sentence can restate the main idea of the paragraph.

   _____

   _____

Editing

5. A fragment lacks a subject or verb and is an incomplete sentence. Identify and correct one fragment.

6. One sentence contains a pronoun shift. The noun and the subsequent pronoun are not consistent. Identify and correct the pronoun shift.

The Writer's Desk **Revise and Edit Your Paragraph**

Revise and edit the paragraph that you wrote for the previous Writer's Desk. Ensure that your paragraph has unity, adequate support, and coherence. Also correct any errors in grammar, spelling, punctuation, and mechanics.

REFLECT ON IT

Think about what you have learned in this chapter. If you do not know an answer, review that topic.

1. What is classification? _____
_____

2. What is the classification principle? _____
_____

3. Give examples of various classification principles that you can use to classify the following items.
   EXAMPLE: Cars *Countries of origin, degrees of fuel efficiency, price*
   a. Animals _____
   b. Sports _____

4. Now choose one classification principle for each item in question 3. Write down three possible categories for that item.
   EXAMPLE: Cars
   Classification principle: *Country of origin*
   Categories: *American cars, European cars, Japanese cars*
   a. Animals
      Classification principle: _____
      Categories: _____
   b. Sports
      Classification principle: _____
      Categories: _____

5. Why is it useful to make a classification chart? _____
_____

The Writer's Room

Topics for Classification Paragraphs

Writing Activity 1

Choose any of the following topics, or choose your own topic. Then write a classification paragraph.

General Topics

Types of . . .

1. parents
2. problems in a relationship
3. friends
4. magazines
5. games
6. sports

College and Work-Related Topics

Types of . . .

7. campus fashions
8. housing
9. roommates
10. bosses
11. office equipment
12. co-workers

Writing Activity 2

Examine this photo, and think about some classification topics. For example, you might discuss types of risky behavior, dangerous jobs, entertainment involving animals, or culturally specific entertainment. Then write a classification paragraph based on the photo or your related topic.

CLASSIFICATION PARAGRAPH CHECKLIST

As you write your classification paragraph, review the checklist on the inside front cover. Also ask yourself the following questions.

- Does my topic sentence explain the categories that will be discussed?

- Do I use a common classification principle to unite the various items?

- Do I offer sufficient details to explain each category?

- Do I arrange the categories in a logical manner?

- Does all of the supporting information relate to the categories that are being discussed?

- Do I include categories that do not overlap?

CHAPTER 10

Comparison and Contrast

Life is often compared to a marathon, but I think it is more like a sprint; there are long stretches of hard work punctuated by brief moments in which we are given the opportunity to perform at our best.

—MICHAEL JOHNSON
American sprinter (b. 1967)

CONTENTS

Shoppers compare prices to obtain the best value for their money. In this chapter, you will practice comparing and contrasting.

EXPLORING

Explore Topics

In the Warm Up, you will try an exploring strategy to generate ideas about different topics.

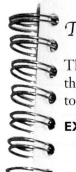

The Writer's Desk **Warm Up**

Think about the following questions, and write down the first ideas that come to your mind. Try to think of two to three ideas for each topic.

EXAMPLE: What are some key features of living alone and living with others?

Living alone

don't have to share

can do what you want whenever

sometimes it's lonely

Living with others

must compromise

share the TV

share the bathroom; schedule
showers

1. What are some key features of high school and college?

   High school

   College

2. What were your goals when you were a child? What are your goals today?

   Goals in childhood

   Goals today

3. Write down the names of two people who are very close to you. You
   might think of friends or family members. Then list some interesting
   characteristics of each person.

   Person 1: _____

   Person 2: _____

What Is Comparison and Contrast?

When you want to decide between options, you compare and contrast. You
compare to find similarities and **contrast** to find differences. The exercise of
comparing and contrasting can help you make judgments about things. It can
also help you better understand familiar things.

   You often compare and contrast. At home, when you watch TV, you might
compare and contrast different programs. At college, you might compare and
contrast different psychological or political theories. On the job, you might need to
compare and contrast computer operating systems, shipping services, or sales figures.

The Comparison and Contrast Paragraph

In a comparison and contrast paragraph, you can compare and contrast two
different subjects, or you can compare and contrast different aspects of a single
subject. For example, you might contrast married life and single life, or you

might write only about marriage but contrast expectations people have before they get married versus what realistically happens after marriage.

When you write a comparison or contrast paragraph, remember to think about your specific purpose.

- **Your purpose could be to make judgments about two things.** For example, you might compare and contrast two restaurants in order to convince your readers that one is preferable.
- **Your purpose could be to describe or understand two familiar things.** For example, you might compare two stories to help your readers understand their thematic similarities.

Comparison and Contrast Patterns

Comparison and contrast texts follow two common patterns. One pattern is to present the details point by point. Another is to present one topic and then the other topic.

When you are thinking about ideas for writing a comparison and contrast paragraph, you can choose one of two methods to organize your supporting ideas: point by point or topic by topic.

ESSAY LINK

To write a comparison and contrast essay, organize *each paragraph* in point-by-point or topic-by-topic form.

Point by Point

Present one point about Topic A and then one point about Topic B. Keep following this pattern until you have a few points for each topic. You go back and forth from one side to the other like tennis players hitting a ball back and forth across a net.

Point A   Point B   Point A   Point B   Point A   Point B

Topic by Topic

Present all points related to Topic A in the first few sentences, and then present all points related to Topic B in the last few sentences. So, you present one side and then the other side, just as lawyers might in the closing arguments of a court case.

All of Topic A   All of Topic B

KYLE'S EXAMPLE

Kyle is trying to decide whether he should take a job in another city or stay at his current job in his hometown. His goal is to decide whether he should move or stay where he is. Kyle could organize his information using a point-by-point or topic-by-topic method.

Point by Point		**Topic by Topic**	
Job A	Low salary	Job A	Low salary
Job B	Good salary		Parents nearby
Job A	Parents nearby		Like my colleagues
Job B	Parents far away		
Job A	Like my colleagues	Job B	Better salary
Job B	Don't know colleagues		Parents far away
			Don't know colleagues

The following *Comparison and Contrast at Work* paragraph uses a point-by-point pattern to contrast two types of people.

Comparison and Contrast at Work

In this paragraph, Dawn Rosenberg McKay, a professional career planner, contrasts a mentor and a protégé.

The mentor is typically more experienced than his or her protégé. He or she possesses the wisdom that only experience can provide. The protégé is someone who is looking to move up the career ladder, usually following in the footsteps of the mentor. The relationship benefits both mentor and protégé. The protégé receives guidance and helpful advice. Invitations to industry events and introductions to industry higher-ups may be forthcoming. The mentor benefits from the opportunity to strengthen his or her leadership skills.

PRACTICE I

Read the next two paragraphs and answer the questions.

A.   Fashion is fashion and teen fashion is meant to shock. According to my son, the girls in his school like to wear decorative thongs and let them peek out from over the tops of their low-slung jeans "for all the boys to see in English class." Their *t*-shirts are tiny, about the size of face cloths. Covering up the back is optional. Oddly, it is my son who finds this style of dressing shocking (among other things). It is not a flattering fashion, for sure, but I dare not complain. In high school I wore a micro miniskirt, and I am sure the boys could see my panties as I climbed the stairs in front of them. I seldom wore a bra (which bothered a friend's father so much, I was not allowed into her house). So, when my son brings home his first near-naked girlfriend, I will not act shocked; I will merely crack a conspiratorial smile.

—Dorothy Nixon, "Teen Fashion"

1. Underline the topic sentence.

2. What aspects of fashion does the author compare? _____

_____

3. What pattern of comparison does the author follow? Circle the correct answer.

   a. Point by point   b. Topic by topic

4. What does this paragraph focus on? Circle the correct answer.

   a. Similarities   b. Differences

B.   Women's sports lag behind men's in media, prize money, and salaries. Some recent comparisons tell the story. The Women's Sport Foundation, a charitable educational organization established in 1974 by Billie Jean King, reports that over ninety percent of all print column inches and hours of televised sports still goes to men's sports. It has only been since 1991 that women's sports received more coverage than horse and dog racing. On the money front, the average prize earnings of the top ten professional male athletes were at least double that of their female counterparts in tennis, bowling, golf, skiing and beach volleyball. There is a huge difference in salaries as well. In professional basketball, the average salary of male players during the 1995–1996 season was 140 times higher than the average salary of female players in the now-**defunct** American Basketball League during its 1996–1997 season. Well, I think you get the picture, and it is not pretty. Now, if we could turn back Father Time and compare the women's games of today to the same developmental period in men's sports, a comparison might seem more legitimate.

defunct: no longer existing

—Ellen Zavian, "Men's and Women's Sports? No Comparison!" *USA Today*

5. Underline the topic sentence.

6. What does this paragraph compare? _____

   _____

7. What pattern of comparison does the author follow? Circle the best answer.

   a. Point by point   b. Topic by topic

8. What does the author focus on? Circle the correct answer.

   a. Similarities   b. Differences

Focus on Similarities, Differences, or Both

After you have chosen a topic and determined your purpose, decide whether you want to focus on comparing (looking at similarities), contrasting (looking at differences), or both. In a paragraph, it is usually best to focus on either comparing or contrasting. In a larger essay, you could more easily do both.

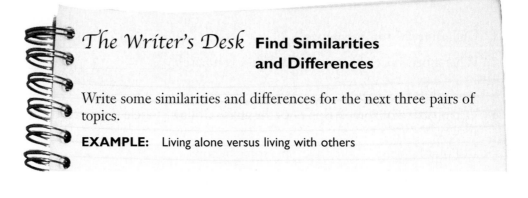

The Writer's Desk **Find Similarities and Differences**

Write some similarities and differences for the next three pairs of topics.

EXAMPLE: Living alone versus living with others

Similarities	**Differences**	
Living alone and with others	Living alone	Living with others
must pay for necessities	have freedom	must compromise
clean up after myself	lonely	people to talk to
learn to balance budget	do all housework	can share jobs
	quiet	others' noise
	expensive	share expenses

I would choose to write a paragraph about ___differences___.

1.
Similarities	**Differences**	
High school and college	High school	College
_____	_____	_____
_____	_____	_____
_____	_____	_____
_____	_____	_____

I would choose to write a paragraph about _____.

2.
Similarities	**Differences**	
Child and adult goals	Childhood goals	Goals today
_____	_____	_____
_____	_____	_____
_____	_____	_____
_____	_____	_____

I would choose to write a paragraph about _____.

3.
Similarities	**Differences**	
Two people who are close to me:	Person 1:	Person 2:
	_____	_____
_____	_____	_____
_____	_____	_____
_____	_____	_____
_____	_____	_____

I would choose to write a paragraph about _____.

ESSAY LINK

In a comparison and contrast essay, the thesis statement expresses the main point of the essay.

DEVELOPING

The Topic Sentence

In a comparison and contrast paragraph, the topic sentence indicates what is being compared and contrasted and expresses a controlling idea.

> Although all dogs make good house pets, large dogs are much more useful than small dogs.

> Topic being compared or contrasted: Large dogs vs. small dogs
> Controlling idea: One is more useful than the other.

PRACTICE 2

Read each topic sentence, and then answer the questions that follow. State whether the paragraph would focus on similarities or differences.

EXAMPLE:

Although coffee and tea can both be caffeinated, tea is a much healthier drink than coffee.

    a. What is being compared? _Coffee and tea_

    b. What is the controlling idea? _One is healthier than the other._

    c. What will the paragraph focus on? Circle the correct answer.

      Similarities   (Differences)

1. Many media pundits complain about reality television; however, reality shows are just as good as regular scripted shows.

    a. What is being compared? _____

      _____

    b. What is the controlling idea? _____

      _____

    c. What will the paragraph focus on? Circle the correct answer.

      Similarities   Differences

2. Before the baby comes, people expect a beautiful world of soft coos and sweet smells, but the reality is quite different.

    a. What is being compared? _____

      _____

    b. What is the controlling idea? _____

      _____

    c. What will the paragraph focus on? Circle the correct answer.

      Similarities   Differences

3. Teenagers are as difficult to raise as toddlers.

    a. What is being compared? _____

       _____

    b. What is the controlling idea? _____

       _____

    c. What will the paragraph focus on? Circle the correct answer.

       Similarities   Differences

The Writer's Desk **Write Topic Sentences**

For each topic, write whether you will focus on similarities or differences. Then, write a topic sentence for each one. You can look for ideas in the Warm Up or in Writer's Desk: Finding Similarities and Differences on pages 130–131. Your topic sentence should include what you are comparing and contrasting, as well as a controlling idea.

Topic: Living alone and living with others

Focus: Differences

Topic sentence: Although many people like the freedom and privacy of living alone, living with other people has its merits.

1. Topic: High school and college

    Focus: _____

    Topic sentence: _____

    _____

2. Topic: Goals in childhood and goals in adulthood

    Focus: _____

    Topic sentence: _____

    _____

3. Topic: Two people who are close to me

    Focus: _____

    Topic sentence: _____

    _____

The Supporting Ideas

After you have developed an effective topic sentence, generate supporting ideas. In a comparison and contrast paragraph, think of examples that help clarify the similarities or differences.

The Paragraph Plan

ESSAY LINK

In a comparison and contrast essay, place the thesis statement in the introduction. Each supporting idea becomes a distinct paragraph with its own topic sentence.

Before you write a comparison and contrast paragraph, it is a good idea to make a paragraph plan. Decide which pattern you will follow: point by point or topic by topic. "**A**" and "**B**" written alongside your topics can indicate which side they support. Then add supporting details. Make sure that each detail supports the topic sentence.

TOPIC SENTENCE: <u>Although many people like the freedom and privacy of living alone, living with other people has its merits.</u>

Point by Point	Topic by Topic
A With others, you can share expenses. **Details:** phone, electricity, etc., costs are less for each person	**A** With others, you can share expenses. **Details:** phone, electricity, etc., costs are less for each person
B Alone, you must pay for everything yourself. **Details:** can be very expensive	**A** With others, there is someone to talk to. **Details:** at end of day, you can discuss experiences
A With others, there is someone to talk to. **Details:** at end of day, you can discuss experiences	**A** With others, you must compromise. **Details:** if there are conflicts, you must find resolution
B Alone, you can sometimes be lonely. **Details:** nobody to come home to	**B** Alone, you must pay for everything yourself. **Details:** can be very expensive
A With others, you must compromise. **Details:** if there are conflicts, you must find resolution	**B** Alone, you can sometimes be lonely. **Details:** nobody to come home to
B Alone, you can do what you want, when you want. **Details:** no worry about making noise	**B** Alone, you can do what you want, when you want. **Details:** no worry about making noise

The Writer's Desk **Write a Paragraph Plan**

Write a detailed paragraph plan in a point-by-point or side-by-side pattern. You can refer to the information you generated in previous Writer's Desk exercises. You can use the letters **A** and **B** to indicate which side you are discussing in your plan. Include details about each supporting idea.

Topic sentence: _____

_____

Support 1: _____

Details: _____

_____

Support 2: _____

Details: _____

_____

Support 3: _____

Details: _____

_____

Support 4: _____

Details: _____

_____

Support 5: _____

Details: _____

_____

Support 6: _____

Details: _____

_____

The First Draft

After you outline your ideas in a plan, you are ready to write the first draft. Remember to write complete sentences. You might include transitional words or expressions to help your ideas flow smoothly.

Transitional Words and Expressions

In comparison and contrast paragraphs, there are some transitional words and expressions that you might use to explain either similarities or differences.

To Show Similarities		To Show Differences	
additionally	in addition	conversely	nevertheless
at the same time	in the same way	however	on the contrary
equally	similarly	in contrast	then again

The Writer's Desk Write the First Draft

Write the first draft of your comparison and contrast paragraph. Before you write, carefully review your paragraph plan to see if you have enough support for your points and topics.

REVISING AND EDITING

Revise and Edit a Comparison and Contrast Paragraph

When you finish writing a comparison and contrast paragraph, carefully review your work and revise it to make the comparison or contrast as clear as possible to your readers. Check that you have organized your paragraph logically, and remove any irrelevant details.

PRACTICE 3

Read the next student paragraph and answer the questions.

Although many people like the freedom and privacy of living alone, living with other people has its merits. When you live alone, there are advantages. For example, you can do what you want when you want, and you do not have to worry about other people's feelings or schedules. However, there are also disadvantages to living alone. You had to pay for everything, and it can be very expensive. It can also be lonely to live alone. At the end of the day, there is nobody to come home to. When you live with others, the advantages are great. You can share expenses of items such as phone and utility bills. Also, you have the warmth of human companionship. Of course, you must make compromises when you share a living space. For example, if your roommate do shift work, you must be quiet when he or she is sleeping. Nonetheless, living with others is preferable to living alone.

Revising

1. In the topic sentence, what is the student comparing or contrasting? _____

   _____

2. What does the writer focus on? Circle the correct answer.
   a. Similarities   b. Differences

3. What pattern does the writer use to organize this paragraph? Circle the correct answer.
   a. Point by point   b. Topic by topic

4. Underline five transitional expressions that appear at the beginning of sentences.

Editing

5. There is one tense inconsistency in the paragraph. Cross out and correct the error.

6. Identify and correct one subject-verb agreement error.

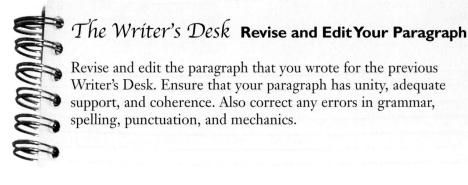

The Writer's Desk **Revise and Edit Your Paragraph**

Revise and edit the paragraph that you wrote for the previous Writer's Desk. Ensure that your paragraph has unity, adequate support, and coherence. Also correct any errors in grammar, spelling, punctuation, and mechanics.

REFLECT ON IT

Think about what you have learned in this chapter. If you do not know an answer, review that topic.

1. Define the words *comparing* and *contrasting*.
   a. Comparing: _____
   b. Contrasting: _____

2. Explain the following comparison and contrast patterns.
   a. Point by point: _____

      _____
   b. Topic by topic: _____

      _____

The Writer's Room   **Topics for Comparison and Contrast Paragraphs**

Writing Activity 1

Choose any of the following topics, or choose your own topic. Then write a comparison and contrast paragraph.

General Topics

Compare or contrast . . .

1. two singers
2. people from two different regions
3. your current home and a home that you lived in before
4. expectations about marriage and the reality of marriage
5. real-life heroes and movie heroes
6. a clean person and a messy person

College and Work-Related Topics

Compare or contrast . . .

7. young college students and older college students
8. two college courses
9. two career options
10. working indoors and working outdoors
11. leaving a child in day care and leaving a child with a family member
12. working mainly with your hands and working mainly with your head

Writing Activity 2

Examine these photos, and think about things that you could compare and contrast. Some ideas might be two types of fashion, two generations, two youth subcultures, or two types of rebellion. Then write a comparison and contrast paragraph.

1920s flappers

James Dean, 1950s rebel

COMPARISON AND CONTRAST PARAGRAPH CHECKLIST

As you write your comparison and contrast paragraph, review the checklist on the inside front cover. Also ask yourself the following questions.

- Does my topic sentence explain what I am comparing and/or contrasting?

- Does my topic sentence make a point about the comparison?

- Does my paragraph have a point-by-point or topic-by-topic pattern?

- Does my paragraph focus on either similarities or differences?

- Do all of my supporting examples clearly relate to the topics that I am comparing or contrasting?

CHAPTER 11

Cause and Effect

" Do not go where the path may lead; go instead where there is no path and leave a trail. "

—RALPH WALDO EMERSON
American essayist and poet (1803–1882)

CONTENTS

Exploring
- Explore Topics
- What Is Cause and Effect?
- The Cause and Effect Paragraph

Developing
- The Topic Sentence
- The Supporting Ideas
- The Paragraph Plan
- The First Draft

Revising and Editing
- Revise and Edit a Cause and Effect Paragraph

What causes dirty air, water, and soil? What are the effects of pollution? Cause and effect writing helps explain the answers to these types of questions.

EXPLORING

Explore Topics

In the Warm Up, you will try an exploring strategy to generate ideas about different topics.

The Writer's Desk Warm Up

Think about the following questions, and write down the first ideas that come to your mind. Try to think of two or three ideas for each topic.

EXAMPLE: Why have governments banned smoking in the workplace?

Secondhand smoke is dangerous for nonsmokers.

Some people have lung problems such as asthma.

Antismoking groups lobby the government for these laws.

1. What are some different ways that people cheat?

_____

_____

_____

2. List a few reasons why some businesses fail.

_____

_____

_____

3. When you were an adolescent, did you rebel in any way? What types of things did you do?

_____

_____

_____

What Is Cause and Effect?

Cause and effect writing explains why an event happened or what the consequences of such an event were. A cause and effect paragraph can focus on causes, effects, or both.

You often analyze the causes or effects of something. At home, you may worry about what causes your siblings or your own children to behave in a certain manner, or you may wonder about the effects of certain foods on your health. In a U.S. history course, you might analyze the causes of the Civil War, or you might write about the effects of industrialization on American society. At work, you may wonder about the effects of a promotion or a pay cut.

The Cause and Effect Paragraph

When you write a cause and effect paragraph, focus on two main points.

1. **Indicate whether you are focusing on causes, effects, or both.** Because a paragraph is not very long, it is often easier to focus on either causes or effects. If you do decide to focus on both causes and effects, make sure that your topic sentence announces your purpose to the reader.

2. **Make sure that your causes and effects are valid.** Determine real causes and effects and do not simply list things that happened before or after the event. Also verify that your assumptions are logical.

Illogical: The product does not work because it is inexpensive.

(This statement is illogical; quality is not always dictated by price.)

Better: The product does not work because it is constructed with poor-quality materials.

The following *Cause and Effect at Work* paragraph discusses causes and effects in a workplace situation.

Cause and Effect at Work

In this memo from the file of a fourth-grade student, early childhood educator Luisa Suarez explains some causes and effects of the child's behavioral and learning problems.

Mark frequently expresses his dislike of school and reading. He continues to read at a second-grade level and is behind his classmates in the acquisition of knowledge expected from fourth-grade students. In interviews with the child, he has stated that he never reads at home and spends most of his time watching television. Because he is so far behind his peers in the classroom, he is embarrassed to show his lack of reading skills for fear of ridicule. It is easier for him to "act out," thus distracting others from his deficiency in reading. He displays a low level of self-confidence and appears to have given up trying.

PRACTICE 1

Read the next paragraph and answer the questions.

When I played football, I learned to be an animal. Being an animal meant being fanatically aggressive and ruthlessly competitive. If I saw an arm in front of me, I trampled it. Whenever blood was spilled, I nodded approval. Broken bones (not mine of course) were secretly seen as little victories within the bigger struggle. The coaches taught me to "punish the other man," but little did I suspect that I was devastating my own body at the same time. There were broken noses, ribs, fingers, toes and teeth, torn muscles and ligaments, bruises, bad knees, and busted lips, and the gradual pulverizing of my spinal column that, by the time my jock career was long over at age 30, had resulted in seven years of near-constant pain. It was a long road to the surgeon's office.

—Don Sabo, "Pigskin, Patriarch, and Pain"

1. Underline the topic sentence.

2. What does this paragraph focus on? Circle the best answer.
   a. Causes   b. Effects

3. Who is the audience? _____

4. List the supporting details.

_____

_____

_____

_____

_____

Identifying Causes and Effects

Imagine that you have to write a cause and effect paragraph about employee absenteeism. You might brainstorm and think of as many causes and effects as possible. Here are some examples:

Causes	Effects
• child is sick	• other employees do more
• employee is sick	• may lose job
• personal problems such as marital strife, depression	• could get demoted
• lack of motivation	• develop financial problems

The Writer's Desk Identify Causes and Effects

Write some possible causes and effects for the following topics. Then decide whether your paragraph will focus on causes or effects.

EXAMPLE: Smoke-free work zones

Causes	Effects
workers complain about smoke	employees smoke in entrances
new legislation	cigarette litter outside building
lobby groups ask for smoke-free zones	smokers influence nonsmokers
	smokers take long breaks
lack of ventilation in offices	

Focus on: _effects_

1. Cheating

Causes	Effects
_____	_____
_____	_____
_____	_____
_____	_____

Focus on: _____

2. Businesses failure

Causes	Effects
_____	_____
_____	_____
_____	_____
_____	_____

Focus on: _____

3. Teenage rebellion

Causes	Effects
_____	_____
_____	_____
_____	_____
_____	_____

Focus on: _____

DEVELOPING

ESSAY LINK

In a cause and effect essay, the thesis statement expresses whether the essay will focus on causes, effects, or both.

The Topic Sentence

The topic sentence in a cause and effect paragraph must clearly demonstrate whether the focus is on causes, effects, or both. Also, make sure that you have clearly indicated your controlling idea. For example, read the topic sentences. Notice that the controlling idea is underlined.

topic   controlling idea (causes)
The Civil War was fought <u>for many reasons</u>.

topic   controlling idea (effects)
The Civil War <u>changed the values</u> of American society in a profound way.

topic   controlling idea (causes and effects)
The Civil War, which was fought <u>for many reasons</u>, <u>changed the</u>
<u>values</u> of American society in a profound way.

PRACTICE 2

Look carefully at the following sets of topic sentences. Decide whether each
sentence focuses on causes, effects, or both. Look for key words that give you
clues, and circle the best answer.

1. My family has suffered serious consequences because of new technology.
   a. Causes   b. Effects   c. Both

2. The Chernobyl nuclear accident led to problems in the environment, as
   well as in people's mental and physical health.
   a. Causes   b. Effects   c. Both

3. The Chernobyl nuclear accident happened due to a lack of safety
   procedures, a faulty design, and poor communication between team
   members.
   a. Causes   b. Effects   c. Both

4. Because of many problems at the Chernobyl nuclear site, the environment
   in the Ukraine has changed forever.
   a. Causes   b. Effects   c. Both

 **Do Not Confuse *Effect* and *Affect***

Generally, *affect* is used as a verb, and *effect* is used as a noun. *Affect* (verb) means
"to influence or change," and *effect* (noun) means "result."

                          verb
   How will the new drug <u>affect</u> pregnant women?

        noun
   What <u>effects</u> will the new drug have on pregnant women?

Effect can also be used as a verb that means "to cause or to bring about." It generally
has the following meanings: "to effect a change" or "to effect a plan."

                              verb
   The union members demonstrated to <u>effect</u> changes in their working conditions.

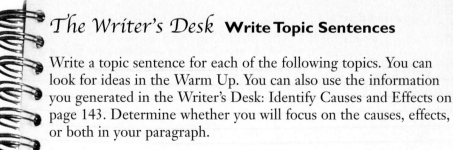

The Writer's Desk **Write Topic Sentences**

Write a topic sentence for each of the following topics. You can
look for ideas in the Warm Up. You can also use the information
you generated in the Writer's Desk: Identify Causes and Effects on
page 143. Determine whether you will focus on the causes, effects,
or both in your paragraph.

EXAMPLE: Smoke-free work zones

Topic sentence: <u>Smoke-free work zones, implemented for obvious reasons, have had surprising consequences for employees.</u>

1. Topic: Cheating

   Topic sentence: _____

   _____

2. Topic: A business failure

   Topic sentence: _____

   _____

3. Topic: Teenage rebellion

   Topic sentence: _____

   _____

The Supporting Ideas

After you have developed an effective topic sentence, generate supporting ideas. When planning a cause and effect paragraph, think of examples that clearly show the causes or effects. Then arrange your examples in emphatic order. **Emphatic order** means that you can place your examples from the most to the least important or from the least to the most important.

 **Do Not Oversimplify**

Avoid attributing a simple or general cause to a complex issue. When you use expressions such as *it appears that* or *a possible cause is*, you show that you are aware of the complex factors involved in the situation.

Oversimplification:	The high murder rate in cities is caused by easily obtained firearms.
	(This is an oversimplification of a complicated problem.)
Better:	A possible cause of the high murder rate in cities is the abundance of easily obtained firearms.

The Writer's Desk **Generate Supporting Ideas**

Choose one of the topic sentences from the Writer's Desk on pages 145–146. Then list either causes or effects.

EXAMPLE: Smoke-free work zones, implemented for obvious reasons, have had surprising consequences for employees.

    polluted entrances of buildings

    smokers need long breaks

    smokers influence nonsmokers

Topic sentence: _____

_____

Supports: _____

_____

_____

_____

The Paragraph Plan

In many courses, instructors ask students to write about the causes or effects of a particular subject. It is a good idea to plan your paragraph before you write your final version. Also think about the order of ideas. Arrange the supporting details in a logical order. As you make your plan, ensure that you focus on causes, effects, or both.

ESSAY LINK

In a cause and effect essay, place the thesis statement in the introduction. Then use body paragraphs, each with its own topic sentence, to support the thesis statement.

TOPIC SENTENCE: Smoke-free work zones, implemented for obvious reasons, have had surprising consequences for employees.

Support 1:   Smokers stand at entrances to have their cigarettes.
   Details: —drop their cigarette butts on the ground
          —heavy smoke at the entrances

Support 2:   Smokers take more breaks.
   Details: —need frequent cigarette breaks
          —not fair to others who must do extra work

Support 3:   Smoking culture influences nonsmokers.
   Details: —nonsmokers take breaks with their smoking friends
          —some nonsmokers become smokers

The Writer's Desk **Write a Paragraph Plan**

Refer to the information you generated in previous Writer's Desk exercises and create a paragraph plan. If you think of new details that will explain your point more effectively, include them here.

Topic sentence: _____

_____

Support 1: _____

    Details: _____

_____

_____

Support 2: _____

    Details: _____

_____

_____

Support 3: _____

    Details: _____

_____

_____

The First Draft

After you outline your ideas in a plan, you are ready to write the first draft. Remember to write complete sentences. You might include transitional words or expressions to help your ideas flow smoothly.

Transitional Words and Expressions

The following transitional expressions are useful for showing causes and effects.

To Show Causes	To Show Effects
for this reason	accordingly
the first cause	as a result
the most important cause	consequently

The Writer's Desk **Write the First Draft**

Write the first draft of your cause and effect paragraph. Before you write, carefully review your paragraph plan and make any necessary changes.

REVISING AND EDITING

Revise and Edit a Cause and Effect Paragraph

When you finish writing a cause and effect paragraph, review your work and revise it to make the examples as clear as possible to your readers. Make sure that your sentences relate to the topic sentence and flow together smoothly.

PRACTICE 3

Read the next student paragraph and answer the questions.

Smoke-free work zones, implemented for obvious reasons, have had surprising consequences for employees. First, smokers light up outside the main entrances of buildings, and nonsmokers must pass through a cloud of heavy smoke to get inside. Additionally, the ground outside entrances is littered with cigarette butts, which smokers do not consider as pollution. Moreover, smokers get more breaks because they frequently leave their workstations to have cigarettes. Some people smoke cigars, and others smoke pipes. The nonsmokers must work more harder to cover for their smoking colleagues, and this makes the nonsmokers resentful. An other surprising consequence is that the smoking culture influences nonsmokers. Former smokers, or those who have never smoked, sometimes get into the habit of smoking in order to socialize with their colleagues during the many breaks. Although no-smoking rules are in the public interest, the consequences of such rules should be examined more thoroughly.

Revising

1. Does the paragraph focus on causes, effects, or both? _____

2. List the causes or effects given. _____

_____

_____

_____

3. There is one sentence in the paragraph that does not really relate to the topic sentence. Cross out that sentence.

Editing

4. There is one error with the comparative form. An adverb is incorrectly formed. Correct the error directly on the text.

5. This paragraph contains two misspelled words. Identify and correct them.

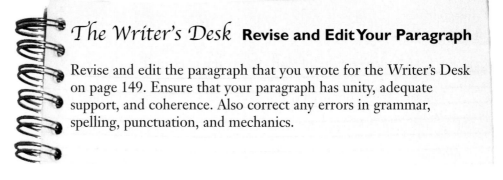

The Writer's Desk **Revise and Edit Your Paragraph**

Revise and edit the paragraph that you wrote for the Writer's Desk on page 149. Ensure that your paragraph has unity, adequate support, and coherence. Also correct any errors in grammar, spelling, punctuation, and mechanics.

REFLECT ON IT

Think about what you have learned in this chapter. If you do not know an answer, review that topic.

1. What is the difference between the words *affect* and *effect?*

    Affect: _____

    Effect: _____

2. Brainstorm to think of three possible causes for each option.

    a. Starting to smoke _____

    _____

    b. A car crash _____

    _____

3. Brainstorm to think of three possible effects for each option.

    a. Pollution: _____

    _____

    b. War: _____

    _____

The Writer's Room   Topics for Cause and Effect Paragraphs

Writing Activity 1

Choose any of the following topics, or choose your own topic. Then write a cause and effect paragraph.

General Topics

Causes and/or effects of . . .

1. having a close friendship
2. having a caffeine addiction
3. getting a higher education
4. having a poor body image
5. spoiling a child
6. joining a sports team

College and Work-Related Topics

Causes and/or effects of . . .

7. having low (or high) marks in college
8. not keeping up with college workload
9. quitting a job
10. working with a family member
11. working at home
12. getting a promotion

Writing Activity 2

Think about a day when you felt frustrated. What causes you to feel like screaming? What are the effects when you scream at someone or when someone screams at you? Write a paragraph about the causes or effects of screaming.

CAUSE AND EFFECT PARAGRAPH CHECKLIST

As you write your cause and effect paragraph, review the checklist on the inside front cover. Also ask yourself the following questions.

- Does my topic sentence indicate clearly that my paragraph focuses on causes, effects, or both?

- Do I have adequate supporting examples of causes and/or effects?

- Do I make logical and valid points?

- Do I use the terms *effect* and/or *affect* correctly?

Argument

"Do not fear to be eccentric in opinion, for every opinion now accepted was once eccentric."

—BERTRAND RUSSELL
British author and philosopher (1872–1970)

Lawyers have to make effective arguments to persuade a judge and jury. In argument writing, you try to convince readers to agree with your point of view.

EXPLORING

Explore Topics

In the Warm Up, you will try an exploring strategy to generate ideas about different topics.

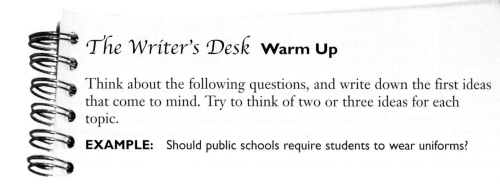

The Writer's Desk Warm Up

Think about the following questions, and write down the first ideas that come to mind. Try to think of two or three ideas for each topic.

EXAMPLE: Should public schools require students to wear uniforms?

Yes, I think so. Then rich kids do not stand out so much, and neither do poor ones. Everyone dresses the same. The kids look more serious. But some kids will hate this rule. They'll try to break the rule somehow.

1. Sometimes minors steal, vandalize, go joyriding, and do other illegal acts. Should parents pay for damages when their children break the law?

   _____

   _____

   _____

2. In some countries, all youths must do two years of military service. What do you think about compulsory military service?

   _____

   _____

   _____

3. What are some of the major controversial issues in your neighborhood, at your workplace, at your college, or in the news these days?

   _____

   _____

   _____

What Is Argument?

When you use **argument,** you take a position on an issue and try to defend your position. You try to convince somebody that your point of view is the best one.

Argument is both a writing pattern and a purpose for writing. In fact, it is one of the most common aims, or purposes, in most college and work-related writing. For example, in Chapter 10, there is a paragraph about teen fashion, and the author uses comparison and contrast as the predominant pattern. At the same time, the author uses argument to convince the reader that fashions have not become more shocking over the years. Therefore, in most of your college and work-related writing, your purpose is to persuade the reader that your ideas are compelling and legitimate.

You use argument every day. You might write a persuasive letter to a newspaper to express your views about public policy. At college, in a sociology class, you might take a position on capital punishment or on gun control. At work, you might have to convince your manager to give you a raise.

Argument at Work

In this memo to a residential program manager, Kamal Natu, a family service worker, uses argument writing to explain why she recommends a children's group home.

My client, a six-year-old boy, should immediately receive part-time placement in a children's group home. He is severely brain damaged and is delayed in every normal area of development, including sensory, social, and emotional functions. He also has a gross deficit in language communication and great difficulties in responding to his enironment. The family needs support to look after him on weekends and during stressful periods. Because of the great demands put on the parents looking after my client, family members cannot enjoy interactions such as eating meals, reading books, playing games, and so on. To relieve some pressure from the family and to look after the boy's needs, weekend placement in a group home for my client is necessary.

The Argument Paragraph

When you write an argument paragraph, remember the following four points.

ESSAY LINK

When you write argument essays, also keep these four points in mind.

- **Choose a subject that you know something about.** It would be very difficult to write a good text about space research funds, capital punishment, or conditions in federal prisons, for example, if you have never had experience with, or read about, these issues. On the other hand, if you, or someone close to you, cannot find good day care, then you could likely write a very effective paper about the necessity of having better day-care services.
- **Consider your readers.** What do your readers already know about the topic? Will they likely agree or disagree with you? Do they have specific concerns? Consider what kind of evidence would be most effective with your audience.
- **Know your purpose.** In argument writing, your main purpose is to persuade the reader to agree with you. Your specific purpose is more focused. You may want the reader to take action, you may want to support a view-point, you may want to counter somebody else's argument, or you may want to offer a solution to a problem. Ask yourself what your specific purpose is.
- **Take a strong position and provide supporting evidence.** The first thing to do in the body of your paragraph is to prove that there is, indeed, a problem. Then back up your point of view with a combination of facts, statistics, examples, and informed opinions.

 **Be Passionate!**

When you are planning your argument paragraph, try to find a topic that you feel passionate about. If you care about your topic, and if you express your enthusiasm, your audience will be more likely to care about it, too.

PRACTICE I

Read the next paragraph and answer the questions.

Ordinary families would benefit greatly from a plan that provided health insurance to those now uninsured. It is true that at any given moment most middle-income families have insurance, but people lose their jobs, companies go bankrupt, and benefits get suddenly slashed. Over any given two-year period, roughly a third of Americans spend some time without health insurance; over longer periods, the risk of losing health insurance is very significant for most families. When a family without health insurance suffers illness, the results are often catastrophic—either serious conditions go untreated or the family faces financial ruin. Our inadequate insurance system is one important reason why America, the richest country in the world, has lower life expectancy and higher child mortality than most other advanced nations. If American families knew what was good for them, then most of them—all but a small, affluent minority—would cheerfully give up any tax cuts in return for a guarantee that health care would be there when needed. And even the affluent might prefer to live in a society where no sick child was left behind.

—Paul Krugman, *New York Times* editorial

1. Underline the topic sentence.

2. Who is the author's audience? _____

3. What is the author's specific purpose? _____

   _____

   _____

4. What health-care issues might concern the audience?

   _____

   _____

   _____

   _____

5. Underline some examples that the author gives to show that there is a problem.

6. Look at the author's supporting evidence, and circle a statistic.

The Topic Sentence

In the topic sentence of an argument paragraph, state your position on the issue.

Topic + Controlling idea (your position on the issue)

controlling idea   topic

<u>Our government should severely punish</u> **corporate executives who commit fraud.**

Your topic sentence should be a debatable statement. It should not be a fact or a statement of opinion.

Fact: In some public schools, students wear uniforms.

(This is a fact. It cannot be debated.)

Opinion: I think that it is a good idea for public school students to wear uniforms.

(This is a statement of opinion. Nobody can deny that you like school uniforms. Therefore, do not use phrases such as *In my opinion, I think,* or *I believe* in your topic sentence.)

Argument: Public school students should wear uniforms.

(This is a debatable statement.)

PRACTICE 2

Evaluate the following statements. Write *F* for a fact, *O* for an opinion, or *A* for a debatable argument.

1. I think that the drinking age is too high in New York State. _____

2. The legal drinking age is too high in New York State. _____

3. The legal drinking age should be lowered to eighteen in all states. _____

4. In Canada, the legal drinking age is eighteen in most provinces. _____

5. In my opinion, some college students drink too much. _____

6. Some students engage in binge drinking on our college campus. _____

7. The proposed "No Binge Drinking" campaign should be scrapped because underage drinking is not a serious problem in our college. _____

8. I believe that most students are responsible and do not abuse alcohol. _____

 **Be Direct**

You may feel reluctant to state your point of view directly. You may feel that it is impolite to do so. However, in academic writing, it is perfectly acceptable, and even desirable, to state an argument in a direct manner.

In argument writing, you can make your topic debatable by using *should, must,* or *ought to* in the topic sentence or thesis statement.

> Although daily prayer is important for many people in the United States, it **should** not take place in the classroom.

The Writer's Desk **Write Topic Sentences**

Write a topic sentence for the next topics. You can look for ideas in the Warm Up on page 153. Make sure that each topic sentence clearly expresses your position on the issue.

EXAMPLE: *Uniforms should be mandatory in public schools.*

1. Topic: Parents paying for children's crime sprees

   Topic sentence: _____

   _____

2. Topic: Compulsory military service

   Topic sentence: _____

   _____

3. Topic: A controversial issue in the news, in your neighborhood, at work, or at college

   Topic sentence: _____

   _____

ESSAY LINK

In an argument essay, body paragraphs should contain supporting details such as examples, facts, informed opinions, logical consequences, or answers to the opposition.

The Supporting Ideas

When you write an argument paragraph, it is important to support your point of view with examples, facts, statistics, and informed opinions. It is also effective to think about some answers you can give to counter the opposition's point of view, and you can consider the long-term consequences if something does not occur. Therefore, try to use several types of supporting evidence.

- **Examples** are pieces of information that illustrate your main argument. For instance, if you want to argue that there are not enough day-care centers in your area, you can explain that one center has over one hundred children on its waiting list.

Another type of example is the **anecdote.** To support your main point, you can write about a true event or tell a personal story. For example, if you think that rebellious teenagers hurt their families, you might tell a personal story about your brother's involvement with a gang.

- **Facts** are statements that can be verified in some way. For example, the following statement is a fact: "According to the World Health Organization, secondhand smoke can cause cancer in nonsmokers." **Statistics** are another type of fact. When you use statistics, ensure that the source is reliable, and remember to mention the source. For example, if you want to argue that underage drinking is a problem, you could mention the following statistic from the *Journal of the American Medical Association:* "Underage drinkers consume about 20 percent of all the alcohol imbibed in this country."

- Sometimes experts in a field express an **informed opinion** about an issue. An expert's opinion can give added weight to your argument. For example, if you want to argue that the courts treat youths who commit crimes too harshly or leniently, then you might quote a judge who deals with juvenile criminals. If you want to argue that secondhand smoke is dangerous, then you might quote a lung specialist or a health organization.

- Solutions to problems can carry **logical consequences.** When you plan an argument, think about long-term consequences if something does or does not happen. For example, in response to the terrorist attacks of September 11, 2001, many governments enacted antiterrorism legislation. However, in some cases, the new laws could be used to suppress legitimate dissent or free speech. Also, those new laws could be misused or misinterpreted by future governments.

- In argument writing, try to **answer the opposition.** For example, if you want to argue that drinking laws are ineffective, you might think about the arguments that your opposition might make. Then you might write, "Drinking age laws do a fine job of keeping young people out of clubs and bars; however, these laws do nothing to keep young people from getting access to alcohol from other places." Try to refute some of the strongest arguments of the opposition.

Hint   Avoid Circular Reasoning

When you write an argument paragraph, ensure that your main point is supported with facts, examples, informed opinions, and so on. Do not use circular reasoning. Circular reasoning means that you restate your main point in various different ways.

Circular	The abundance of spam is not harmless; in fact, a lot of junk e-mail is offensive. People receive many copies of junk mail and the content offends them. Most people complain when they receive too much junk e-mail, and they feel especially unhappy when the junk e-mail has offensive images.
Not Circular	The abundance of spam is not harmless; in fact, a lot of junk e-mail is offensive. According to Odin Wortman of Internet Working Solutions, about thirty percent of e-mail is pornographic. Children and older people open such mail hoping for a message from a friend, only to see an offensive picture. Another thirty percent of junk mail advertises fraudulent schemes to get rich quick and hawks products of questionable value or safety.

PRACTICE 3

You have learned about different methods to support a topic. Read each of the following topic sentences and think of a supporting reason for each item. Use the type of support suggested in parentheses.

1. Boys should be encouraged to express their emotions.

    (Logical Consequence) _____

    _____

    _____

2. Unleashed dogs should not be allowed on public streets.

    (Example) _____

    _____

    _____

3. The attendance policy at this college is (or is not) effective.

    (Fact) _____

    _____

    _____

4. Teen magazines should not show ads with extremely thin models.

    (Logical Consequence) _____

    _____

    _____

5. When a couple goes on a date, the person who earns the most money should always pay the bill.

    (Answer the opposition.) _____

    _____

    _____

RESEARCH LINK

For more information about avoiding plagiarism and evaluating and documenting sources, refer to Chapter 15, "Enhancing Your Writing with Research."

Hint **Using Research**

You can enhance your argument essay with **research** by including information from an informed source. You could look for information in textbooks, newspapers, magazines, and on the Internet.

When you use the Internet for research, make sure that your sources are from legitimate organizations or from reputable magazines, newspapers, or government sites. For example, for information about the spread of AIDS, you might find statistics on the World Health Organization's Web site. You would not go to someone's personal rant or conspiracy theory site.

Consider Both Sides of the Issue

Once you have decided what to write about, try to think about both sides of the issue. Then you can predict arguments that your opponents might make, and you can plan your answer to the opposition.

EXAMPLE: Uniforms in public schools

For
—students will look serious in school
—students will not be judged on their fashion
—equalizes the look of poor and rich kids
—is economical: three uniforms cost less than a wardrobe of the latest fashions

Against
—students will lose sense of individuality
—parents and students may resist
—some parents cannot afford to buy uniforms
—students might compare school to a prison

The Writer's Desk **Consider Both Sides of the Issue**

Write arguments for and against each of the following topics.

1. Parents should pay for children's crimes.

   For   **Against**

   _____   _____

   _____   _____

   _____   _____

   _____   _____

2. Military service should be compulsory.

   For   **Against**

   _____   _____

   _____   _____

   _____   _____

   _____   _____

3. A controversial issue: _____

   For   **Against**

   _____   _____

   _____   _____

   _____   _____

   _____   _____

Hint   Avoid Common Errors

When you write an argument paragraph or essay, avoid the following pitfalls.

Do not make generalizations. If you begin a statement with *Everyone knows* or *It is common knowledge*, then the reader may mistrust what you say. You cannot possibly know what everyone else knows. It is better to refer to specific sources.

Generalization:	Everyone knows that sending troops to Iraq was necessary.
Better:	Prominent politicians such as Donald Rumsfeld stated that sending troops to Iraq was necessary.

Use emotional arguments sparingly. Certainly, the strongest arguments can be emotional ones. Sometimes the most effective way to influence others is to appeal to their sense of justice, humanity, pride, or guilt. However, do not rely on emotional arguments. If you use emotionally charged words (for example, if you call someone *ignorant*) or if you try to appeal to base instincts (for example, if you appeal to people's fear of other ethnic groups), then you will seriously undermine your argument.

Emotional:	Bleeding-heart liberals did not want the United States to send troops to Iraq.
Better:	Many sectors of society, including several student activists, actors, educators, and business groups, did not want the United States to send troops to Iraq.

Do not make exaggerated claims. Make sure that your arguments are plausible.

Exaggerated:	If military forces had not captured Iraq's leader, Saddam Hussein, eventually the United States would have been destroyed.
Better:	If military forces had not captured Saddam Hussein, the tyrant would have continued to terrorize his people.

The Paragraph Plan

Before you write your argument paragraph, make a plan. Think of some supporting arguments, and think about details that can help illustrate each argument. Ensure that every example is valid and that it relates to the topic sentence. Also, arrange your ideas in a logical order.

TOPIC SENTENCE:	There should be mandatory uniforms in public schools.
Support 1:	Students will feel as if they belong.
Details:	—Uniforms will give a sense that students are united.
Support 2:	Uniforms will equalize rich and poor students.
Details:	—Rich students cannot show off their expensive clothing. —Poor students will not stand out so much.
Support 3:	Uniforms are convenient.
Details:	—Instead of a large wardrobe, two or three uniforms serve for school. —Students do not waste time deciding what to wear each day.

The Writer's Desk Write a Paragraph Plan

Choose one of the topic sentences that you wrote for the Writer's Desk on page 158, and write a detailed paragraph plan. You can refer to the information you generated in previous Writer's Desk exercises, and if you think of examples that will explain your point more effectively, include them here.

Subject: _____

Topic sentence: _____

_____

Support 1: _____

Details: _____

_____

Support 2: _____

Details: _____

_____

Support 3: _____

Details: _____

_____

The First Draft

After you outline your ideas in a plan, you are ready to write the first draft. Remember to write complete sentences. You might include transitional words or expressions to help your ideas flow smoothly.

Transitional Words and Expressions

The following transitional words and expressions can introduce an answer to the opposition or the support for an argument.

To Answer the Opposition	To Support Your Argument
admittedly	certainly
however	consequently

(continued)

To Answer the Opposition	To Support Your Argument
nevertheless	furthermore
of course	in fact
on one hand/on the other hand	obviously
undoubtedly	of course

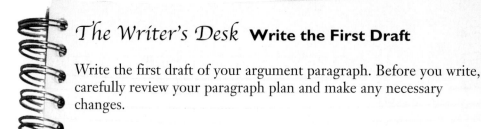

The Writer's Desk **Write the First Draft**

Write the first draft of your argument paragraph. Before you write, carefully review your paragraph plan and make any necessary changes.

REVISING AND EDITING

Revise and Edit an Argument Paragraph

When you finish writing an argument paragraph, carefully review your work and revise it to make the supporting examples as clear as possible to your readers. Check that the order of ideas is logical, and remove any irrelevant details.

PRACTICE 4

Read the next student paragraph and answer the questions.

> In public schools, some students wear inappropriate clothing such as low-cut jeans and dirty baseball caps, and they look idiotic. To solve the problem, there should be mandatory uniforms in public schools. When schools make uniforms compulsory, most students develop a stronger sense of loyalty to their school. With uniforms, rich students are no longer able to display their wealth by wearing expensive clothing, and poor students do not need to buy the latest fashions. Nobody would feel no pressure to have brand-name clothing. School uniforms are also convenient and less costly. Students would no longer have to spend money on a large wardrobe, and two or three uniforms could serve for the whole school year. Also, students are gonna waste less time deciding what to wear each day. If schools do not make uniforms compulsory, students will wear bathing suits to school, and the corridors could become filled with anarchy. Definitely it is a good idea to force students to wear school uniforms.

Revising

1. Underline the topic sentence. Remember that the topic sentence is not always the first sentence in the paragraph.

2. The writer uses emotionally charged words and exaggerates. Give examples of each of these problems.

   Emotionally charged word: _____

   Exaggeration: _____

   _____

3. List the three arguments that support the topic sentence.

   _____

   _____

   _____

Editing

4. In this paragraph there is one nonstandard verb, which is a verb that people say but should not write. Underline the error and write the correct form in the space below.

   Correction: _____

5. This paragraph contains a double negative. Underline the error and write the correct phrase in the space.

   Correction: _____

The Writer's Desk Revise and Edit Your Paragraph

Revise and edit the paragraph that you wrote for the previous Writer's Desk. Ensure that your paragraph has unity, adequate support, and coherence. Also correct any errors in grammar, spelling, punctuation, and mechanics.

REFLECT ON IT

Think about what you have learned in this chapter. If you do not know an answer, review that topic.

1. What is the main purpose of an argument paragraph or essay?

   _____

2. What is the difference between a statement of opinion and a statement of argument?

   _____

   _____

(continued)

3. What five types of supporting evidence can you use in argument writing?

_____   _____

_____   _____

_____   _____

4. In argument writing, you should avoid circular reasoning. What is circular reasoning?

_____

_____

5. Why is it important to avoid using emotionally charged words?

_____

_____

 The Writer's Room   **Topics for Argument Paragraphs**

Writing Activity 1

Choose any of the following topics, or choose your own topic. Then write an argument paragraph. Remember to narrow your topic and to follow the writing process.

General Topics

1. fame
2. the voting age
3. disciplining children
4. chat room relationships
5. alternative medical therapies
6. body image

College and Work-Related Topics

7. drug testing
8. value of a college education
9. compulsory physical education in college
10. longer vacations for workers
11. office relationships
12. affirmative action

Writing Activity 2

Examine the photo, and think about arguments that you might make about marriage. For example, you might argue about the high cost of weddings, the best type of wedding, why people should or should not marry, or the benefits of premarital counseling. Then write an argument paragraph.

✓ ARGUMENT PARAGRAPH CHECKLIST

As you write your argument paragraph, review the checklist on the inside front cover. Also ask yourself the following questions.

☐ Does my topic sentence clearly state my position on the issue?

☐ Do I make strong supporting arguments?

☐ Do I include facts, examples, statistics, logical consequences, or answers to the opposition?

☐ Do my supporting arguments provide evidence that directly supports the topic sentence?

PART III

The Essay

What Is an Essay?

An essay is a series of paragraphs. Essays differ in length, style, and subject, but the structure of an essay generally consists of an *introductory paragraph,* several *body paragraphs,* and a *concluding paragraph.*

Before you begin reading the next chapters, become familiar with the parts of the common five-paragraph essay.

Each body paragraph begins with a topic sentence.

The introductory paragraph introduces the essay's topic and contains its thesis statement.

The title gives a hint about the essay's topic.

The thesis statement contains the essay's topic and its controlling idea.

Alternative Culture

In an era when alternative has become mainstream, what's an angst-ridden teenager to do? Dying hair punk colors has become passé. Goths with white face powder, dark lipstick, and lots of eyeliner no longer attract even a second glance. Everyone listens to "alternative" music. It has become increasingly hard for a teenager to rebel against the mainstream.

In other eras, youths had something to rebel about. The 1960s had the hippie era, as young adults rebelled by protesting against injustice, the Vietnam War, and the restrictions of society. LSD, marijuana, and free love reigned. Flash forward to the 1970s, when the punk movement came into existence with bands such as the Sex Pistols, and unemployed youths railed against consumerism. Kurt Cobain in the early 1990s became the rallying cry for a new generation of teenagers disillusioned with the confines of society. But what about now?

Furthermore, bizarre fashion statements have become acceptable. Previously, rebellious teenagers had to resort to shopping in thrift stores or making their own clothes to attain their desired fashion statement. Luckily (or unluckily) for them, society now makes it easy to dress like an individual. Companies make jeans that already have holes in them so they do not have to wait around to have that punk look. If they want to look different, they can try Urban Outfitters, the trendy chain store for people who are fed up with trendy chain stores, where they can look "unique" just like everone else who shops there.

With this watering down of alternative culture, it has become harder and harder to shock anyone or gain any notorious press. Marilyn Manson, the press's former whipping boy and scapegoat for music as a cause of violence in society (witness the aftermath of the Columbine shootings), has faded from the public's view. Then Eminem became a strange symbol for the increasingly difficult quest to be different from everyone else and to shock society into paying attention. He got some press for his song about killing his wife, but today, nobody is paying attention.

Perhaps to be truly alternative, adolescents must think for themselves. They must be themselves, no matter what they might be. They can dress as punk or as preppy as they like. They should not let society's version of "alternative" control their actions. The truly cool can think for themselves.

The concluding paragraph brings the essay to a satisfactory close.

Each body paragraph contains details that support the thesis statement.

—*Veena Thomas, student*

Writing the Essay

66 Without words, without writing, and without books there would be no history, and there could be no concept of humanity. 99

—HERMANN HESSE
German author (1877–1962)

Completed in 1973, The Sydney Opera House in Australia has tons of concrete, steel, and glass supporting its structure. In the same way, an essay is a sturdy structure that is supported by a strong thesis statement and solid body paragraphs held together by plenty of facts and examples.

EXPLORING

Explore Topics

There are limitless topics for writing essays. Your knowledge and personal experiences will help you find topics and develop ideas when you write your essay.

When you are planning your essay, consider your topic, audience, and purpose. Your **topic** is who or what you are writing about. Your **audience** is your intended reader, and your **purpose** is your reason for writing. Do you hope to entertain, inform, or persuade the reader?

Narrowing the Topic

Your instructor may assign you a topic for your essay, or you may need to think of your own. In either case, you need to narrow your topic (make it more specific) to ensure that it suits your purpose for writing and fits the size of the assignment. To narrow your topic, you can use some exploring methods such as questioning or brainstorming.

When you narrow your topic, keep in mind that an essay contains several paragraphs; therefore, an essay topic can be broader than a paragraph topic. In the next examples, you will notice that the essay topic is narrow but is slightly larger than the paragraph topic.

Broad Topic	**Paragraph Topic**	**Essay Topic**
Job interview	Dressing for the interview	Preparing for the interview
Rituals	College orientation week	Initiation rituals

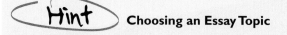

> ### Hint   Choosing an Essay Topic
>
> Paragraphs and essays can also be about the same topic. However, an essay has more details and concrete examples to support its thesis.
>
> Do not make the mistake of choosing an essay topic that is too broad. Essays that try to cover a large topic risk being superficial and overly general. Make sure that your topic is specific enough that you can cover it in an essay.

OCTAVIO NARROWS HIS TOPIC

Student writer Octavio Sanchez used both brainstorming and questioning to narrow his broad topic, "live entertainment." His audience was his English instructor, and the purpose of his assignment was to persuade.

- should beautiful old theaters be restored?
- ban street performers
- permit artists to sell portraits on the streets
- why clowns are creepy
- bad circuses
- treatment of circus animals
- what is talent?
- the best types of nightclubs

The Writer's Desk Narrow the Topics

Practice narrowing five broad topics.

EXAMPLE:

Money: – reasons it doesn't make you happy

    – teach children about value of money

    – best ways to be financially successful

1. Crime: _____

_____

_____

2. Volunteer work: _____

_____

_____

3. Fashion: _____

_____

_____

4. Advertising: _____

_____

_____

5. Education: _____

_____

_____

DEVELOPING

The Thesis Statement

Once you have narrowed the topic of your essay, develop your thesis statement. The **thesis statement**—like the topic sentence in a paragraph—introduces the topic of the essay and arouses the interest of the reader.

Characteristics of a Good Thesis Statement

A thesis statement has three important characteristics.

- It expresses the main topic of the essay.
- It contains a controlling idea.
- It is a complete sentence that usually appears in the essay's introductory paragraph.

Here is an example of an effective thesis statement.

topic   controlling idea
Marriage has lost its importance for many young people in our society.

Writing an Effective Thesis Statement

When you develop your thesis statement, ask yourself the following questions.

1. **Is my thesis statement a complete statement that has a controlling idea?**
   Your thesis statement should always reveal a complete thought and make a point about the topic. It should not announce the topic or express a widely known fact.

Incomplete:	Gambling problems.
	(This statement is not complete.)
Announcement:	I will write about lotteries.
	(This statement announces the topic but says nothing relevant about the topic. Do not use expressions such as *I will write about . . .* or *My topic is . . .*)
Thesis statement:	A lottery win will not necessarily lead to happiness.

2. **Does my thesis statement make a valid and supportable point?** Your thesis statement should express a valid point that you can support with evidence. It should not be a vaguely worded statement, and it should not be a highly questionable generalization.

Vague:	Workplace relationships are harmful.
	(For whom are they harmful?)
Invalid point:	Women earn less money than men.
	(Is this really true for all women in all professions? This generalization might be hard to prove.)
Thesis statement:	Before co-workers become romantically involved, they should carefully consider possible problems.

3. **Can I support my thesis statement in an essay?** Your thesis statement should express an idea that you can support in an essay. It should not be too broad or too narrow.

Too broad:	There are many museums in the world.
	(It would be difficult to write an essay about this topic.)
Too narrow:	The Spy Museum is in Washington.
	(What more is there to say?)
Topic sentence:	Washington's Spy Museum contains fascinating artifacts related to the secret world of espionage.

Hint **Give Specific Details**

Give enough details to make your thesis statement interesting. Your instructor may want you to guide the reader through your main points. To do this, mention both your main point and your supporting points in your thesis statement. In other words, your thesis statement provides a map for the readers to follow.

Weak:	My first job taught me many things.
Better:	My first job taught me about responsibility, organization, and the importance of teamwork.

PRACTICE I

Identify the problem in each thesis statement. Then revise each statement to make it more interesting and complete.

Announces	Invalid	Broad
Incomplete	Vague	Narrow

EXAMPLE:

I will write about human misery on television news.

Problem: *Announces*

Revised statement: *Television news programs should not treat personal tragedies as big news.*

1. I think that college friendships are important.

   Problem: _____

   Revised statement: _____

   _____

2. Scholarships go to athletes, so academic excellence is not appreciated in colleges.

   Problem: _____

   Revised statement: _____

   _____

3. Scientific discoveries have changed the world.

   Problem: _____

   Revised statement: _____

   _____

4. The streets are becoming more dangerous.

   Problem: _____

   Revised statement: _____

   _____

5. How to discipline children.

   Problem: _____

   Revised statement: _____

   _____

6. This essay will talk about security and privacy on the Internet.

   Problem: _____

   Revised statement: _____

   _____

The Writer's Desk **Write Thesis Statements**

For each item, choose a narrowed topic from the Writer's Desk on page 170. Then write an interesting thesis statement. Remember that each thesis statement should contain a controlling idea.

EXAMPLE: Topic: Money

Narrowed topic: _Winning a lottery_

Thesis statement: _Rather than improving your life, a lottery win can lead to feelings of guilt, paranoia, and boredom._

1. Topic: Crime

   Narrowed topic: _____

   Thesis statement: _____

   _____

2. Topic: Volunteer work

   Narrowed topic: _____

   Thesis statement: _____

   _____

3. Topic: Fashion

   Narrowed topic: _____

   Thesis statement: _____

   _____

4. Topic: Advertising

   Narrowed topic: _____

   Thesis statement: _____

   _____

5. Topic: Education

   Narrowed topic: _____

   Thesis statement: _____

   _____

The Supporting Ideas

The thesis statement expresses the main idea of the entire essay. In the following illustration, you can see how the ideas flow in an essay. Topic sentences relate to the thesis statement, and details support the topic sentences; therefore, every single idea in the essay is unified and supports the thesis.

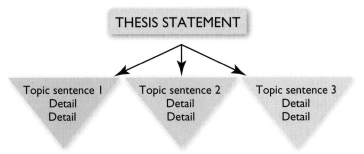

PRACTICE 2

Read the following essay. After you have finished reading, do the following:

1. Create an effective thesis statement. It should sum up the point of the entire essay.

2. Write a topic sentence at the beginning of each body paragraph. The topic sentence should sum up the main point of the paragraph in an interesting way.

Introduction:

Danger has always been synonymous with travel. In past centuries, pirates on the high seas attacked passing ships. Land travelers were not much safer; bandits could attack their covered carriages. Even trains were not safe; in 1877 the masked outlaw Sam Bass held up a train in Nebraska and robbed the passengers. Today, with modern communication and with high-speed trains and planes, travel is quick and relatively risk-free. Nonetheless, there are still certain hazards inherent in traveling.

Thesis statement: _____

_____

Body paragraph 1 topic sentence: _____

_____

For example, before you arrive in a new town, find an address and phone number for affordable lodging, and book a room for your first night. If you are a budget traveler, you can always find cheaper accommodations the next day. If you are going to visit a large city, plan to arrive during the daylight hours. It is dangerous to arrive at night and then try to find your way around. Also, make sure that you have a map of your destination. You can download maps on the Internet.

Body paragraph 2 topic sentence: _____

_____

Do not flash your money in public places. You might wear a money belt under your clothing. One innovative solution is to sew long, extended pockets on the insides of your clothes; you could keep your checks and passport there. In a small, easily accessible purse or wallet, keep small amounts of local currency for your daily spending.

Body paragraph 3 topic sentence: _____

_____

For example, you could bring along a first aid kit that includes bandages and pain relievers. Wear hats in very hot, sunny places. If you are visiting a tropical country, make sure you have the proper vaccinations. Be careful about where you eat and what you eat, and buy bottled drinking water. Your health is important. Obviously, if you get sick, you are not going to enjoy your trip.

Conclusion:

Although robberies can happen, it is unlikely that someone will physically hurt you. If you take risks with your health, if you are careless with your money and passports, or if you underestimate thieves, you may have an unpleasant experience. Of course, if you are careful, you should have a perfectly safe and exciting trip.

Generating Supporting Ideas

An effective essay has **unity** when the body paragraphs support the thesis statement. When you develop supporting ideas, make sure that they all focus on the central point that you are making in the thesis statement. To generate ideas for body paragraphs, you could use exploring strategies such as brainstorming, clustering, or freewriting.

OCTAVIO'S SUPPORTING IDEAS

Octavio created a list to support his thesis statement. Then he reread his supporting points and removed ideas that he did not want to develop in his essay.

THESIS STATEMENT: Circuses should be banned from using large animals such as tigers, bears, and elephants.

Supporting points:

— animals may get hurt in training and during the show

— tigers may be muzzled or even drugged

— whips and electric prods are used on animals

— animals are a danger to public and trainers

— ~~not good education for children~~

— some animals go on rampages

— animals are kept in confined spaces

— moved around in hot trailers or trains

— no room to roam

— ~~circus animals are not that interesting to see~~

The Writer's Desk **List Supporting Ideas**

Choose two of your thesis statements from the previous Writer's Desk on page 174, and create two lists of possible supporting ideas.

Thesis 1: _____   Thesis 2: _____

_____   _____

Support: _____   Support: _____

_____   _____

_____   _____

_____   _____

_____   _____

_____   _____

_____   _____

_____   _____

_____   _____

_____   _____

_____   _____

Organizing Your Ideas

After you have examined your list of supporting ideas, choose three or four that are most compelling and most clearly support your statement. Highlight your favorite ideas, and then group together related ideas. Finally, make your essay as clear and coherent as possible by organizing your ideas in a logical manner using time, space, or emphatic order.

OCTAVIO'S EXAMPLE

Octavio underlined his three best supporting points, and he grouped related ideas using emphatic order.

2
- animals may get hurt in training and during the show
- dangerous animals may be muzzled or even drugged
- whips and electric prods are used on animals

3
- animals are a danger to public and trainers
- not good education for children
- some animals go on a rampage

1
- animals are kept in confined spaces
- moved around in hot trailers or trains
- no room to roam
- circus animals are not that interesting to see

The Writer's Desk **Organize Your Ideas**

Look at the list you produced in the previous Writer's Desk, and then follow these steps.

1. Highlight at least three ideas from your list that you think are most compelling and most clearly illustrate the point you are making in your thesis statement.

2. Group together any related ideas with the three supporting ideas.

3. Organize your ideas using time, space, or emphatic order.

The Essay Plan

An **essay plan** or an **outline** can help you organize your thesis statement and supporting ideas before writing your first draft. To create an essay plan, follow these steps.

- Look at your list of ideas and identify the best supporting ideas.
- Write topic sentences that express the main supporting ideas.
- Add details under each topic sentence.

In the planning stage, you do not have to develop your introduction and conclusion. It is sufficient to simply write your thesis statement and an idea for your conclusion. Later, when you develop your essay, you can develop the introduction and conclusion.

OCTAVIO'S ESSAY PLAN

Octavio wrote topic sentences and supporting examples and organized his ideas into a plan. Notice that he begins with his thesis statement, and he indents his supporting ideas.

THESIS STATEMENT:	<u>Circuses should be banned from using large animals such as tigers, bears, and elephants.</u>
Body paragraph 1:	Travel is hard on the animals. —They are moved around in hot trailers or trains. —They are kept in small cages.
Body paragraph 2:	Animals may get hurt in training or during the show. —Tigers and bears are muzzled or drugged. —Trainers use electric prods and whips.
Body paragraph 3:	The animals are a danger to the public and trainers. —Some animals go on rampages. —Some attack and kill their trainers.
Concluding idea:	Circuses do not need wild animals in order to be successful.

Writing a Formal Essay Plan

Most of the time, a basic essay plan is sufficient. However, in some of your courses, your instructor may ask you to make a formal plan. A formal plan uses Roman numerals and letters to identify main and supporting ideas.

Thesis statement: _____

    I. _____

        A. _____

        B. _____

   II. _____

        A. _____

        B. _____

  III. _____

        A. _____

        B. _____

Concluding idea: _____

PRACTICE 3

Create an essay plan based on Veena Thomas's essay "Alternative Culture" on page 168.

_____

_____

_____

_____

_____

_____

_____

_____

_____

_____

_____

_____

_____

PRACTICE 4

Complete the following essay plan. Add details under each supporting point. Make sure that the details relate to the topic sentence.

Thesis statement: Rather than improving your life, a lottery win can lead to feelings of guilt, paranoia, and boredom.

I.   Feelings of guilt are common in newly rich people.

Details: A._____

_____

B._____

_____

C._____

_____

II. Lottery winners often become paranoid.

Details: A._____

_____

B._____

_____

C._____

_____

III. After lottery winners quit their jobs, they commonly complain of boredom.

Details: A._____

_____

B._____

_____

C._____

_____

Concluding idea: _____

_____

_____

The Writer's Desk **Write an Essay Plan**

Write an essay plan using one of your thesis statements and supporting details you came up with in the previous Writer's Desk on page 178.

Thesis statement: _____

_____

I. _____

Details: A. _____

B. _____

C. _____

II. _____

Details: A. _____

B. _____

C. _____

III. _____

Details: A. _____

B. _____

C. _____

Concluding idea: _____

_____

The Introduction

After you have made an essay plan, you develop the sections of your essay by creating an effective introduction, linking paragraphs, and a conclusion.

The **introductory paragraph** introduces the subject of your essay and contains the thesis statement. A strong introduction will capture the reader's attention and make him or her want to read on. Introductions may have a lead-in, and they can be developed in several different ways.

The Lead-In

You can begin the introduction with an attention-grabbing opening sentence, or lead-in. There are three common types of lead-ins.

- Quotation
- Surprising or provocative statement
- Question

Introduction Styles

You can develop the introduction in several different ways. Experiment with any of these introduction styles.

- **Give general or historical background information.** The general or historical information gradually leads to your thesis. For example, in an essay about winning a lottery, you could begin by giving a brief history of lotteries.
- **Tell an interesting anecdote.** Open your essay with a story that leads to your thesis statement. For example, you might begin your lottery essay by telling the story of a real-life lottery winner.
- **Present a vivid description.** Give a detailed description, and then state your thesis. For example, you might describe the moment when a lottery winner realizes that he or she has won.
- **Present an opposing position.** Open your essay with an idea that contradicts a common belief, and build to your thesis. For instance, if most people want to win the lottery, you could begin your essay by saying that you definitely do not want to be a millionaire.
- **Give a definition.** Define a term, and then state your thesis. For example, in an essay about the lottery, you could begin by defining *happiness.*

Hint ▸ **Placement of the Thesis Statement**

Although a paragraph often begins with a topic sentence, an introduction does not begin with a thesis statement. Rather, most introductions begin with sentences that introduce the topic and lead the reader to the main point of the essay. In other words, the thesis statement is generally the last sentence in the introduction.

PRACTICE 5

In introductions A through E, the thesis statement is underlined. Read each introduction and then answer the questions that follow. Look at Octavio's example for some guidance.

OCTAVIO'S INTRODUCTION

"Welcome to the greatest show on earth!" The ringmaster's voice echoes through the circus tent. In the arena, a majestic elephant lifts itself onto its hind legs and walks carefully toward its trainer. The crowd murmurs with appreciation, unaware that the elephant may be an unwilling, neglected, or even abused participant in this spectacle. <u>Circuses should be banned from using large animals such as tigers, bears, and elephants.</u>

1. What type of lead-in does Octavio use? *Quotation*

2. What introduction style does he use?
   - (a.) Description
   - b. Definition
   - c. Background information
   - d. Opposing position

3. What is his essay about? *Abolishing the use of large animals in circuses*

A. "I never saw the blow to my head come from Huck. Bam! And I was on all fours, struggling for my equilibrium." These are the words of Kody Scott, a former member of a Los Angeles street gang. Kody is describing part of the initiation ritual he endured in order to join a local branch (or "set") of the Crips. First, he stole an automobile to demonstrate his "street smarts" and willingness to break the law. Then he allowed himself to be beaten, showing both that he was tough and that he was ready to do whatever the gang required of him. He completed the process by participating in a "military action"—killing a member of a rival gang. <u>Initiations like this are by no means rare in today's street gangs.</u> Kody, by the way, was just eleven years old.

> —Linda L. Lindsey and Stephen Beach, "Joining the Crips," *Essentials of Sociology*

1. What type of lead-in does the author use? _____

2. What introduction style does the author use?
    a. Anecdote   b. Definition
    c. Background information   d. Opposing position

3. What is this essay about? _____

B. What is there about alternative medicine that sets it apart from ordinary medicine? The term refers to a remarkable heterogeneous group of theories and practices that are as disparate as homeopathy, therapeutic touch, imagery, and herbal medicine. What unites them? Eisenberg et al. defined alternative medicine (now often called complementary medicine) as "medical interventions not taught widely at U.S. medical schools or generally available at U.S. hospitals." <u>That is not a very satisfactory definition, especially since many alternative remedies have recently found their way into the medical mainstream.</u>

> —Adapted from Marcia Angell and Jerome P. Kassirer, "Alternative Medicine: The Risks of Untested and Unregulated Remedies," *The New England Journal of Medicine*

4. What type of lead-in does the author use? _____

5. What introduction style does the author use?
    a. Anecdote   b. Definition
    c. Description   d. Opposing position

6. What is this essay about? _____

C. High school is a waste of time. In fact, it is a baby-sitting service for teens who are too old to be baby-sat. In England, fifteen-year-olds graduate and can choose technical or university streams of education. They are free to choose what to study, or they can stop schooling and get jobs. In short, they are treated like mature adults. In our country, we prolong the experience of forced schooling much longer than is necessary. <u>We should abolish high schools and introduce a system of technical or pre-university schooling.</u>

> —Adelie Zang, Student

7. What type of lead-in does the author use? _____

8. What introduction style does the author use?
   a. Anecdote   b. Definition
   c. Background information   d. Opposing position

9. What is this essay about? _____

D. When I was 8 years old, I read a story about a boy who built a robot out of junkyard scraps. The robot in the story could move, talk, and think, just like a person. For some reason, I found the idea of building a robot very appealing, so I decided to build one of my own. I remember optimistically collecting body parts: pipes for arms and legs, motors for muscles, light bulbs for eyes, and a big tin can for the head, fully expecting to assemble the pieces into a working mechanical man. After nearly electrocuting myself a few times, I began to get my parts to move, light up, and make noises. I felt I was making progress. <u>If I only had the right tools and the right parts, I was sure that I could build a machine that could think.</u>

—Danny Hillis, "Can They Feel Your Pain?"

10. What introduction style does the author use?
    a. Anecdote   b. Definition
    c. Background information   d. Opposing position

11. What is this essay about? _____

E. The story of how Christianity ultimately conquered the Roman Empire is one of the most remarkable in history. Christianity faced the hostility of the established religious institutions of its native Judea and had to compete not only against the official cults of Rome and the sophisticated philosophies of the educated classes, but also against "mystery" religions like the cults of Mithra, Isis, and Osiris. <u>The Christians also suffered formal persecution, yet Christianity finally became the official religion of the empire.</u>

—Albert M. Craig et al., *The Heritage of World Civilizations*

12. What introduction style does the author use?
    a. Description   b. Definition
    c. Historical information   d. Opposing position

13. What is this essay about? _____

The Writer's Desk Write Two Introductions

In the previous Writer's Desk on page 181, you made an essay plan. Now, write two different styles of introductions for your essay. Use the same thesis statement in both introductions. Later, you can choose the best introduction for your essay.

The Conclusion

A **conclusion** is a final paragraph that rephrases the thesis statement and summarizes the main points in the essay. To make your conclusion more interesting and original, you could close with a prediction, a suggestion, a quotation, or a call to action.

OCTAVIO'S CONCLUSION

Octavio concluded his essay by restating his main points.

> Clearly, large animals suffer when they are enclosed, carted around from town to town, and forced to perform for crowds of humans. Perhaps traditional circuses should consider the example of Cirque du Soleil, which does not use any large animals in its shows, yet it is one of the world's most profitable and popular circuses.

He could then close his essay with one of the following:

Prediction:	If animal-free circuses continue to thrive, then perhaps we will see a day when lions, tigers, elephants, and bears are not forced to perform in circus rings.
Suggestion:	The best way to change practices of circuses is to avoid those that use large animals.
Quotation:	According to Mahatma Gandhi, "A nation's moral progress can be judged by the way it treats its animals."
Call to action:	If you feel strongly about the use of large animals in circuses, you could write letters about the issue to local and state politicians.

PRACTICE 6

Read the following conclusions and answer the questions.

> A. As soon as smoking is banned in all public places, we will see the benefits. Our hospitals will treat fewer smoking-related illnesses, and this will save money. Non-smokers will be saved from noxious fumes, and smokers, who will be forced to smoke outdoors, might feel a greater desire to give up the habit. In the future, we will have a world where a non-smoker can go through life without having to breathe in someone else's cigarette smoke.
>
> —Jordan Lamott, "Butt Out!"

1. What method does the author use to end the conclusion?
   a. Prediction   b. Suggestion
   c. Quotation   d. Call to action

> B. Ultimately, spam is annoying, offensive, time consuming, and expensive. There is nothing good to say about it. Spam marketers will argue that we get junk in our mail, and that cannot be denied, but we

do not get crates of junk mail every week. If we did, paper junk mail would be banned in a hurry. The only real solution is for governments around the world to work together in order to make spam production illegal. Governments must actively hunt down and prosecute spammers.

—Adela Fonseca, "Ban Spam"

2. What method does the author use to end the conclusion?

a. Prediction   b. Suggestion

c. Quotation   d. Call to action

C. Every once in a while the marketing wizards pay lip service to today's expanding career options for women and give us a Scientist Barbie complete with a tiny chemistry set as an accessory. But heaven forbid should little Johnnie plead for his parents to buy him that Scientist Barbie. After all, it is acceptable for girls to foray, occasionally, into the world of boy-style play, but for boys the opposite "sissified" behavior is taboo. Why is this? One commentator, D. R. Shaffer, says, "The major task for young girls is to learn how not to be babies, whereas young boys must learn how not to be girls."

—Dorothy Nixon, "Put GI Barbie in the Bargain Bin"

3. What method does the author use to end the conclusion?

a. Prediction   b. Suggestion

c. Quotation   d. Call to action

Hint **Avoiding Conclusion Problems**

In your conclusion, do not contradict your main point, and do not introduce new or irrelevant information.

The Writer's Desk **Write a Conclusion**

In previous Writer's Desks, you wrote an introduction and an essay plan. Now write a conclusion for your essay.

The First Draft

After creating an introduction and conclusion, and after arranging the supporting ideas in a logical order, you are ready to write your first draft. The first draft includes your introduction, several body paragraphs, and your concluding paragraph.

The Writer's Desk **Write the First Draft**

In previous Writer's Desks, you wrote an introduction, a conclusion, and an essay plan. Now write the first draft of your essay.

REVISING AND EDITING

Revising and Editing the Essay

Revising your essay is an extremely important step in the writing process. When you revise your essay, you modify it to make it stronger and more convincing. You do this by reading the essay critically, looking for faulty logic, poor organization, or poor sentence style. Then you reorganize and rewrite it, making any necessary changes.

Editing is the last stage in writing. When you edit, you proofread your writing and make sure that it is free of errors.

Revising for Unity

To revise for **unity,** verify that all of your body paragraphs support the thesis statement. Also look carefully at each body paragraph: ensure that the sentences support the topic sentence.

> **Hint** **Avoiding Unity Problems**
>
> Here are two common errors to check for as you revise your body paragraphs.
>
> - **Rambling paragraphs**   The paragraphs in the essay ramble on. Each paragraph has several topics, and there is no clearly identifiable topic sentence.
>
> - **Artifical breaks**   A long paragraph is split into smaller paragraphs arbitrarily, and each smaller paragraph lacks a central focus.
>
> To correct either of these errors, revise each body paragraph until it has *one* main idea that supports the thesis statement.

Revising for Adequate Support

When you revise for adequate **support,** ensure that there are enough details and examples to make your essay strong and convincing.

Revising for Coherence

When you revise for **coherence,** ensure that paragraphs flow smoothly and logically. To guide the reader from one idea to the next, or from one paragraph to the next, try using **paragraph links.**

You can develop connections between paragraphs using three methods.

1. **Repeat words or phrases from the thesis statement in each body paragraph.** In the next example, *violent* and *violence* are repeated words.

Thesis statement:	Although some will argue that <u>violent</u> movies are simply a reflection of a <u>violent</u> society, these movies actually cause a lot of the <u>violence</u> around us.
Body paragraph 1:	Action movie heroes train children to solve problems with <u>violence</u>.
Body paragraph 2:	<u>Violent movies</u> are "how to" films for many sick individuals.

2. **Refer to the main idea in the previous paragraph, and link it to your current topic sentence.** In body paragraph 2, the writer reminds the reader of the first point (the newly rich feel useless) and then introduces the next point.

Thesis statement:	A cash windfall may cause more problems than it solves.
Body paragraph 1:	The newly rich often lose their desire to become productive citizens, and they end up <u>feeling useless</u>.
Body paragraph 2:	Apart from <u>feeling useless</u>, many heirs and lottery winners also tend to feel guilty about their wealth.

3. **Use a transitional word or phrase to lead the reader to your next idea.**

Body paragraph 2:	<u>Furthermore</u>, the newly rich often feel guilty about their wealth.

OCTAVIO'S ESSAY

Octavio examined his essay to see if it had unity, adequate support, and coherence. Review the notes that Octavio made in the margin of his essay.

"Welcome to the greatest show on earth!" The ringmaster's voice echoes through the circus tent. In the arena, a majestic elephant lifts itself onto its hind legs and walks carefully toward its trainer. The crowd murmurs with appreciation, unaware that the elephant may be an unwilling, neglected, or even abused participant in this spectacle. <u>Circuses should be banned from using large animals such as tigers, bears, and elephants.</u>

Add transition: First?

<u>Large animals are kept in tiny, confined spaces.</u> On circus grounds, large animals are restrained in small cages where they barely have room to lie down. When the animals travel, they are confined to hot trailers or trains, and sometimes they must spend days in such conditions.

Needs more details.

<u>Animals may get hurt in training and during the show.</u> While preparing the animals for the show, trainers use electric prods and whips. <u>It is important that trainers be dominant.</u> Trainers want to show the animals that they are in control, but trainers often hurt animals during practice exercises.

Add transition: Furthermore?

Unity: does this idea belong?

Large circus animals are a danger to the public and to enter-tainers. In some circuses, elephants have gone on rampages and attacked or even killed others. Tigers have turned on trainers. After such attacks happen, people wonder why the animals suddenly turned wild. Wild animals are not meant to be performing pets.

Clearly, large animals suffer when they are enclosed, carted around from town to town, and forced to perform for crowds of humans. Perhaps traditional circuses should consider the example of Cirque du Soleil, which does not use any large animals in its shows, yet it is one of the world's most profitable and popular circuses. If animal-free circuses continue to thrive, then perhaps we will see a day when lions, tigers, elephants, and bears are not forced to perform in circus rings.

Add link?

Needs specific example.

Is the order logical?

Is this a good example? Are there more?

Revising for Style

Another important step in the revision process is to ensure that you have varied your sentences and that you have used concise wording. When you revise for sentence style, ask yourself the following questions.

- Do I use a variety of sentence patterns?
- Do I use exact language?
- Are my sentences parallel in structure?

Editing

When you edit, you proofread your essay and correct any errors in punctuation, spelling, grammar, and mechanics. There is an editing guide on the inside back cover of this book that provides you with a list of things to check for when you proofread your text.

The Writer's Desk **Revising and Editing Your Essay**

In the previous Writer's Desk in this chapter, you wrote the first draft of an essay. Now revise and edit your essay. You can refer to the checklist at the end of this chapter.

The Essay Title

It is a good idea to think of a title after you have completed your essay because then you will have a more complete impression of your essay's main point. The most effective titles are brief, depict the topic and purpose of the essay, and attract the reader's attention.

When you write your title, place it at the top center of your page. Capitalize the first word of your title, and capitalize the main words except for prepositions (*in, at, for, to,* etc.) and articles (*a, an, the*). Leave about an inch of space between the title and the introductory paragraph.

Descriptive Titles

Descriptive titles are the most common titles in academic essays. They depict the topic of the essay clearly and concisely. Sometimes, the author takes key words from the thesis statement and uses them in the title. Here are some descriptive titles.

The Importance of Multiculturalism in a Democratic Society

Why Mothers and Fathers Should Take Parenting Seriously

Titles Related to the Writing Pattern

You can also relate your title directly to the writing pattern of your essay. Here are examples of titles for different writing patterns.

Illustration:	The Problems with Elections
Narration:	My Visit to Las Vegas
Description:	Graduation Day
Process:	How to Dress for an Interview
Definition:	What It Means to Be Brave
Classification:	Three Types of Hackers
Comparison and contrast:	Fast Food vs. Gourmet Food
Cause and effect:	Why People Enter Beauty Pageants
Argument:	Barbie Should Have a New Look

 **Hint** **Avoiding Title Pitfalls**

When you write your title, watch out for problems.

• Do not view your title as a substitute for a thesis statement.

• Do not put quotation marks around the title of your essay.

• Do not write a really long title because it can be confusing.

PRACTICE 7

1. List some possible titles for the essay about travel in Practice 2 (page 175).

_____

_____

2. List some possible titles for Octavio's essay about circus animals (page 188).

_____

_____

The Final Draft

When you have finished making the revisions on the first draft of your essay, write the final copy. This copy should include all the changes that you have made during the revision phase of your work. You should proofread the final copy of your work to check for grammar, spelling, mechanics, and punctuation errors.

The Writer's Desk   Writing Your Final Draft

At this point, you have developed, revised, and edited your essay. Now write the final draft. Before you hand it to your instructor, proofread it one last time to ensure that you have found as many errors as possible.

REFLECT ON IT

Think about what you have learned in this unit. If you do not know an answer, review that topic.

1. What is a thesis statement? _____

   _____

2. What are the five different introduction styles?

   _____   _____

   _____   _____

   _____

3. What are the four different ways to end a conclusion?

   _____   _____

   _____   _____

4. What are the three different ways you can link body paragraphs?

   _____

   _____

   _____

The Writer's Room   Essay Topics

Writing Activity 1

Choose any of the following topics, or choose your own topic. Then write an essay. Remember to follow the writing process.

General Topics

1. values
2. having a roommate
3. differences between generations
4. violence
5. peer pressure

College and Work-Related Topics

6. juggling college and family life
7. having a job and going to college
8. extracurricular activities at college
9. a stressful work environment
10. an important issue in the workplace

REVISING AND EDITING CHECKLIST FOR ESSAYS

Revising

☐ Does my essay have a compelling introduction and conclusion?

☐ Does my introduction have a clear thesis statement?

☐ Does each body paragraph contain a topic sentence?

☐ Does each body paragraph's topic sentence relate to the thesis statement?

☐ Does each body paragraph contain specific details that support the topic sentence?

☐ Do all of the sentences in each paragraph relate to its topic sentence?

☐ Do I use transitions to smoothly and logically connect ideas?

☐ Do I use a variety of sentence styles?

Editing

☐ Do I have any errors in grammar, spelling, punctuation, and capitalization?

Essay Patterns

CHAPTER 14

" *The act of writing is the act of discovering what you believe.* "

—David Hare
American playwright (1947–)

Fashion designers choose fabric patterns that are appropriate for the articles of clothing that they wish to make. In the same way, writers choose essay patterns that best suit their purposes for writing.

In Chapters 4 through 12, you read about and practiced using nine different paragraph patterns. In this chapter, you will learn how to apply those patterns when writing essays. Before you begin working through this chapter, take a moment to review nine writing patterns.

Pattern	Definition
Illustration	To illustrate or prove a point using specific examples
Narration	To narrate or tell a story about a sequence of events that happened
Description	To describe using vivid details and images that appeal to the reader's senses
Process	To inform the reader about how to do something, how something works, or how something happened
Definition	To define or explain what a term or concept means by providing relevant examples
Classification	To classify or sort a topic to help readers understand different qualities about that topic

(continued)

Pattern	Definition
Comparison and contrast	To present information about similarities (compare) or differences (contrast)
Cause and effect	To explain why an event happened (the cause) or what the consequences of the event were (the effects)
Argument	To argue or to take a position on an issue and offer reasons for your position

Most college essay assignments have one dominating essay pattern. However, you can use several essay patterns to fulfill your purpose. For example, imagine that you want to write a cause and effect essay about youth crime, and the purpose of the essay is to inform. The supporting paragraphs might include a definition of youth crime and a narrative about an adolescent with a criminal record. You might incorporate different writing patterns, but the dominant pattern would still be cause and effect.

Each time you write an essay, remember to follow the writing process that you learned in Chapter 13, "Writing the Essay."

PARAGRAPH LINK

For more information about developing ideas with examples, refer to Chapter 4, "Illustration."

The Illustration Essay

When writing an illustration essay, you use specific examples to illustrate or clarify your main point. Illustration writing is a pattern that you frequently use in college essays and exams because you must support your main idea with examples.

The Thesis Statement

The thesis statement in an illustration essay controls the direction of the body paragraphs. It includes the topic and a controlling idea about the topic.

topic   controlling idea

A second language <u>provides students with several important advantages</u>.

The Supporting Ideas

In an illustration essay, the body paragraphs contain examples that support the thesis statement. You can develop each body paragraph in two different ways. To give your essay variety, you could use both a series of examples and extended examples.

- **Use a series of examples** that support the paragraph's topic sentence. For example, in an essay about bad driving, one body paragraph could be about drivers who do not pay attention to the road. The paragraph could list the things that those drivers do, such as looking through CDs, using a cell phone, eating, and putting on makeup.

- **Use an extended example** to support the paragraph's topic sentence. The example could be an anecdote or a description of an event. In an essay about bad driving, for example, one paragraph could contain an anecdote about a driver who always wanted to be faster than other drivers.

An Illustration Essay Plan

Read the next essay plan and answer the questions.

Introduction
Thesis statement: New technologies have had a profound impact on self-employed workers.

I. Hand-held organizers help such workers maintain a portable office.
   A. stores e-mails, schedules, phone lists, and more
   B. models are lightweight and fit in a pocket
   C. messenger services provide means to communicate in real time

II. Portable computers provide workers with the ability to do complicated things anywhere.
   A. can format and design documents using graphs, tables, and art
   B. can write, revise, and edit simultaneously
   C. no need to carry large paper files; computers can store hundreds of files
   D. can access Internet while traveling

III. Computer printers have useful features for the self-employed worker.
   A. integrated scanners and photocopiers
   B. fax machine allows easy sending and receiving of messages
   C. laser printers can quickly print out large volumes of documents

Conclusion: As technologies evolve, more people will work at home.

PRACTICE I

1. Circle the topic and underline the controlling idea in the thesis statement.

2. How does the writer develop each body paragraph? Circle the best answer.
   a. With an extended example   b. With a series of examples

3. Write another topic sentence that could support the writer's thesis statement.

   _____

   _____

An Illustration Essay

Read the next essay by journalist Stephen Lautens and answer the questions.

Down Time

1   As I write this, my phone is ringing. I am also doing my Internet banking and refilling the fax machine with paper. How did we all get so busy? We eat our breakfast and check our voice mail on the drive to work. The ATM line is the perfect place to call an estranged relative or answer our pager. What we have done is successfully eliminated the concept of spare time. It seems like we are not happy unless we have filled every waking moment of our lives with something to do.

2   My father knew how to relax. I remember him sitting on the big green couch under a reading lamp for hours at a time, carefully going through the newspaper. It was as if time stood still. Sometimes he would just listen to music. It is amazing because all he was doing was listening to music—not trying to balance his checkbook and make a stock trade at the same time.

3   Some of my best times as a kid were days when I had nothing planned. Nothing was sweeter than the first day of the vast summer holiday, without a single thing to fill it. My mother tried **valiantly** to send us off to camp, but I refused to go. I took goofing around very seriously. Much to my mother's dismay, I never had any interest in hockey, soccer, or any other organized sport that made me get up early or lose any teeth.

4   Technology has given us some terrific benefits, but now we feel that we are wasting valuable time unless we are doing six things at once. I am not knocking vaccines, airbags, or NSYNC CDs, but there is something wrong when everyone has to have a website. (I am guilty as charged.) We feel we have to be an expert on the high-tech stocks—otherwise how can we expect to be a dot-com millionaire by the age of twelve? Electronic appointment books are being marketed for children so they can schedule their play dates. No doubt they can also keep track of all the other six-year-olds' e-mail addresses and cell phone numbers. There is a TV commercial on right now where a little boy puts his playmates on a conference call, which is probably good practice for the day when he has to eat his lunch at his desk with a phone in his ear.

5   Now when I get a few days off, it is so packed with errands and obligations that I am worn out by Monday morning. Maybe it is just part of growing up. If it is, I do not recommend it to anyone. Do not get me wrong. I like to be busy, but we have forgotten the need to slow down. We feel the need to be connected all the time. So go ahead. Turn off the phone and have a nap. I guarantee the world will still be there when you wake up, and it will look better too.

valiantly: bravely

PRACTICE 2

1. Underline the thesis statement of the essay.

2. Underline the topic sentence in each body paragraph.

3. In which paragraph(s) does the author make an extended example?

    _____

4. In which paragraph(s) does the author list ideas to illustrate his point?

    _____

5. What suggestion does the author make in the conclusion of the essay?

    _____

    _____

The Writer's Room

Topics for Illustration Essays

PARAGRAPH LINK

You could also develop an essay about one of the topics found in Chapter 4, "Illustration."

Writing Activity 1

Write an illustration essay about one of the following topics.

General Topics

1. the junk in your home
2. characteristics of a good friend
3. entertainment activities
4. useless products or inventions
5. accomplishments of a cultural icon
6. commercialization of holidays

College and Work-Related Topics

7. reasons to take time off before starting college
8. qualities of an ideal workplace
9. skills that you need for your job
10. qualities of co-workers who are easy or difficult to get along with
11. important things to know about doing your job
12. your employment history

Writing Activity 2

Read the following quotations. Find one that you agree or disagree with, or find one that inspires you in some way. Then write an illustration essay based on the quotation.

Sports serve society by providing vivid examples of excellence.
—George F. Will, American editor and columnist

After climbing a great hill, one only finds that there are many more hills to climb.
—Nelson Mandela, former South African president

Everything has its beauty, but not everyone sees it.
—Confucius, ancient Chinese philosopher and educator

Everyone I meet is in some way my superior.
—Ralph Waldo Emerson, American author

Creativity comes from looking for the unexpected and stepping outside your experience. Computers simply cannot do that.
—Masaru Ibuka, Japanese businessman

✔ ILLUSTRATION ESSAY CHECKLIST

As you write your illustration essay, review the essay checklist on the inside front cover. Also ask yourself the following questions.

☐ Does my thesis statement include a topic that I can support with examples?

☐ Does my thesis statement make a point about the topic?

(continued)

> Do my body paragraphs contain sufficient examples that clearly support the thesis statement?
>
> Do I smoothly and logically connect the examples?

PARAGRAPH LINK

For more information about narrative writing, refer to Chapter 5, "Narration."

The Narrative Essay

When you write a narrative essay, you tell a story about what happened, and you generally explain events in the order in which they occurred.

There are two main types of narrative writing. In **first-person narration,** you describe a personal experience using *I* or *we*. In **third-person narration,** you describe what happened to somebody else, and you use *he, she,* or *they*.

The Thesis Statement

The thesis statement controls the direction of the body paragraphs. To create a meaningful thesis statement for a narrative essay, you could ask yourself what you learned, how you changed, or how the event is important.

controlling idea   topic

<u>Something terrible happened</u> **that summer I turned fifteen.**

The Supporting Ideas

Here are some tips to remember as you develop a narrative essay.

- Make sure that it has a point. Do not simply recount what happened. Try to indicate why the events are important.
- Organize the events in time order (the order in which they occurred). You could also reverse the order of events by beginning your essay with the outcome of the events, and then explaining what happened that led to the outcome.
- Make your narrative essay more interesting by using some descriptive language. For example, you could use images that appeal to the senses.

To be as complete as possible, a good narrative essay should provide answers to most of the following questions.

- *Who* is the essay about?
- *What* happened?
- *When* did it happen?
- *Where* did it happen?
- *Why* did it happen?
- *How* did it happen?

> ⟨ **Hint** ⟩ **Using Quotations**
>
> One effective way to enhance your narrative essay is to use dialogue. Include direct and/or indirect quotations.
>
> A **direct quotation** contains the exact words of an author, and the quotation is set off with quotation marks. When you include the exact words of more than one person, you must start a new paragraph each time the speaker changes.
>
> Sara looked at me sadly. "Why did you betray me?"
>
> "I didn't mean to do it," I answered.
>
> She looked down at her hands and said, "I don't think I can ever forgive you."
>
> An **indirect quotation** keeps the author's meaning but is not set off by quotation marks.
>
> Sara asked why I had betrayed her.

A Narrative Essay Plan

Read the next essay plan and answer the questions that follow.

Introduction

Thesis statement: Stephen Glass, a promising young writer in Washington, D.C., shocked the world of journalism with his fabricated stories.

I. After his first small falsehood, his lying escalated.
    A. invented a quotation in 1995
    B. invented sources to back up his stories
    C. knew about fact checkers, so he created false memos, meeting notes, etc.
    D. soon entire stories filled with lies

II. Glass's career came to a crashing end.
    A. *Forbes* magazine wanted to follow up a Glass story about hackers
    B. Glass unable to produce documents about sources
    C. invented more lies to cover up his initial lies
    D. realizing Glass was unethical, editor of *New Republic* fired him in 1998

III. The Glass scandal erupted, shocking publishers and readers.
    A. story became front-page news
    B. editors' competency was questioned
    C. fact checkers exposed as not being thorough enough
    D. readers wondered if journalists could be trusted

Conclusion: The world of journalism is still recovering from the Glass scandal.

PRACTICE 3

1. Who is this essay plan about? _____

2. What happened? _____

3. When and where did this happen? _____

4. What type of narration is this? Circle the best answer.
   a. First person   b. Third person

A Narrative Essay

In the next essay, Jeff Kemp recounts what happened during his early years as a professional football player. Read the essay and answer the questions.

A Lesson in Humility

1   We live in an age when, too often, rules are scorned, values are turned upside down, principles are replaced by **expediency,** and character is sacrificed for popularity. Individual athletes are sometimes the worst offenders, but not as often as one might think. In fact, sports teach important moral lessons that athletes can apply on and off the playing field.

expediency: convenience; self-interest

2   Many people dream of being a professional athlete. For me, the dream seemed to be within reach because my father, Jack Kemp, an outstanding quarterback, played for the American Football League's Buffalo Bills (prior to the AFL's 1970 merger with the National Football League). The trouble was, I was not very good! I was a third-string football player through most of junior high and high school and for two years at Dartmouth College. I was not anyone's idea of a "hot prospect." After graduation, I was passed over by NFL scouts. When I finally was asked to join the Los Angeles Rams in 1981 as a free agent, I was **designated** as fifth-string quarterback.

designated: selected

3   It was a 50-to-1 shot that I would survive training camp. Rookies were the only players required to show up for the first week of camp. There were dozens competing for the few spots open on the team. After two days, a young boy approached me as I was walking off the field. He asked if he could carry my helmet to the locker room. It was a long way, but I said, "Sure, I think you can handle that." The next morning, he showed up before practice and offered to carry my helmet and shoulder pads, and he was there again after practice offering the same service. So it went for the rest of the week.

4   On the last day, as we were departing the field, my young assistant said, "Jeff, can I ask you a question?" (We were on a first-name basis by then.)

5   I thought, "This is my first fan! He is going to ask me for an autograph."

6   He then inquired, "When do the good football players come to camp?" Right then and there, I learned a lesson in humility from a seven-year-old boy.

7   In my first three NFL seasons, I was forced to learn the same lesson over and over again. During that time, I threw just 31 passes. Nevertheless, by 1984, I had managed to outlast the five NFL quarterbacks who had been ahead of

me. With the Rams' record standing at 1–2, I took over for injured quarterback Vince Ferragamo and earned my first start against the Cincinnati Bengals, eventually leading the Rams to nine more victories and a playoff berth.

8   The next season, I returned to the bench as a backup quarterback. Humility, I was compelled to remind myself, was a good thing. It helped me appreciate what I had and avoid dwelling on what I did not have. It prevented complaining, which drains the spirit and unity of any group. It also led me to persevere and be ready whenever opportunity presented itself.

PRACTICE 4

1. What type of narration is this text? Circle the best answer.
   a. First person   b. Third person

2. Underline the thesis statement of the essay.

3. What introduction style does Kemp use? Circle the best answer.
   a. Definition   b. Anecdote
   c. General information   d. Historical information

4. List the main events that Kemp recounts in his essay.

   _____

   _____

   _____

   _____

   _____

   _____

   _____

5. What organizational method does Kemp use? Circle the best answer.
   a. Time order   b. Space order   c. Emphatic order

6. Write down one example of an indirect quotation from the essay.

   _____

7. Write down one example of a direct quotation from the essay.

   _____

8. Narrative writers do more than simply list a series of events. Kemp explains why the events were meaningful. What did Kemp learn?

   _____

   _____

PARAGRAPH LINK

You could also develop one of the topics found in Chapter 5, "Narration."

 The Writer's Room   **Topics for Narrative Essays**

Writing Activity I

Write a narrative essay about one of the following topics.

General Topics

1. a family legend
2. an illuminating moment
3. a surprising coincidence
4. a poor financial decision
5. an important event in the world
6. when you learned to do something new

College and Work-Related Topics

7. life lessons that college teaches you
8. what your previous job taught you
9. your best or worst job
10. a good or bad experience with a bank
11. when you worked with a team
12. a scandal at work or college

Writing Activity 2

Read the following quotations. Find one that you agree or disagree with, or find one that inspires you in some way. Then write a narrative essay based on the quotation.

Drama is life with the dull bits cut out.

—Alfred Hitchcock, British filmmaker

When your mouth stumbles, it's worse than feet.

—Oji proverb

Those who cannot remember the past are condemned to repeat it.

—George Santayana, Spanish poet and philosopher

If you tell the truth, then you don't have to remember everything.

—Mark Twain, American author

We can draw lessons from the past, but we cannot live in it.

—Lyndon B. Johnson, American politician

✓ NARRATIVE ESSAY CHECKLIST

As you write your narrative essay, review the essay checklist on the inside front cover. Also ask yourself the following questions.

☐ Does my thesis statement clearly express the topic of the narration, and does it make a point about that topic?

☐ Does my essay answer most of the following questions: *who, what, when, where, why, how?*

☐ Do I use transitional expressions that help clarify the order of events?

☐ Do I include details to make my narration more interesting?

The Descriptive Essay

When writing a descriptive essay, use words to create a vivid impression of a subject. Use details that appeal to the five senses: sight, smell, hearing, taste, and touch. You want your readers to be able to imagine all that you are describing.

PARAGRAPH LINK

For more information about descriptive writing, refer to Chapter 6, "Description."

The Thesis Statement

In a descriptive essay, the thesis statement includes what you are describing and makes a point about the topic.

topic   controlling idea
Walking down the streets of New York, I was filled with a sense of wonder.

The Supporting Ideas

When you develop your descriptive essay, make sure it has a **dominant impression.** The dominant impression is the overall feeling that you wish to convey. For example, the essay could convey an impression of tension, joy, nervousness, or anger.

You can place the details of a descriptive essay in space order, time order, or emphatic order. The order that you use depends on the topic of your essay. For example, if you describe a place, you can use space order, and if you describe a difficult moment, you can use time order.

Hint **Using Figurative Devices**

When writing a descriptive essay, you can use figurative devices such as simile, metaphor, or personification. These devices use comparisons and images to add vivid details to your writing.

• A **simile** is a comparison using *like* or *as*.

Just imagine me with no flaws
like a parking lot with no cars . . .   —Mya, "Movin' On"

My son's constant whining felt like a jackhammer on my skull.

• A **metaphor** is a comparison that does not use *like* or *as*.

I'm a genie in a bottle . . .   —Christina Aguilera, "Genie in a Bottle"

The mind is a battlefield.

• **Personification** is the act of attributing human qualities to an inanimate object or animal.

The wind kicked the leaves.   —Kurt Vonnegut, Jr., "Next Door"

The sauce hissed on the stove.

PRACTICE 5

Practice using figurative language. Use one of the following to describe each item: simile, metaphor, or personification. If you are comparing two things, try to use an unusual comparison.

EXAMPLE:

Surprising: _Her sudden appearance was as surprising as a 4 a.m. phone call. (simile)_

1. Truck: _____

2. Road: _____

3. Crowd: _____

4. Annoying: _____

5. Relaxed: _____

A Descriptive Essay Plan

Read the next essay plan and answer the questions that follow.

Introduction

Thesis statement: Walking down the streets of Manhattan, I was filled with a sense of wonder.

I. Times Square was buzzing with bright lights, bustling crowds, and eclectic sounds.
   A. the lights on the billboards
   B. the theaters on every corner
   C. the chatter of many different languages
   D. the salty pretzels on my tongue

II. Central Park was an oasis in the center of Manhattan
   A. the joggers on the running paths
   B. the hansom drivers with their beautiful horses
   C. the smell of the hot dogs and sausages
   D. the saxophone player, the bird lady, and the mime

III. Battery Park, on the southern tip of the island, was impressive.
   A. the roar of the waves crashing
   B. the chilly wind on my face
   C. the Statue of Liberty in the distance
   D. the shouts of the vendors

Conclusion: "Outside America, New York is America, and its skyscraper a symbol of the spirit of America" (Thomas Adams, 1931).

PRACTICE 6

1. This essay plan contains imagery that appeals to the senses. Find one example of imagery for each sense.

   a. Sight: _____

   _____

b. Sound: _____

_____

c. Smell: _____

_____

d. Taste: _____

_____

e. Touch: _____

_____

2. Which type of imagery is most prevalent? _____

3. What is the dominant impression of this essay? Circle the best answer.
   a. Desire   b. Suspicion
   c. Joy and awe   d. Sadness

A Descriptive Essay

Read the following essay by Rahul Goswami, a journalist for *Orientation: Middle East*, and answer the questions. Pay close attention to the descriptive details.

Monsoon Time

1   My father used to tell me about the **monsoon** in Bangladesh. He was born in Handiyal, a village in the north-central district of the country. Behind his parents' house was a river, the Padma, a part of the immense water system that crisscrosses Bangladesh. Big even during the sweltering dry months, the Padma would become an inland ocean at the height of the monsoon. My father would talk about the river swelling day after day as the rain drove down. He loved the monsoon, despite the inevitable annual floods, the misery, and the hardship.

monsoon: rainy season in South Asia

2   Years later, I moved to Dubai, where I lived until just recently. It is a modern metropolis—built on the edge of the great Arabian sand sea—glittering with glazed glass and proud of its impeccably maintained highways. It **scarcely** ever rains here. On perhaps five days a year, a few millimeters of rain will reluctantly descend. More frequent are the sandstorms, which clog drains that are tested no more than annually. This past year was my first full one in Dubai and the first time in my life I have missed an entire monsoon.

scarcely: hardly; rarely

3   By June in India, when the first wet **squalls** explode over Bombay, one has been anticipating the rain for a month and more. Then in July, the massive, heavy cloud systems have settled immovably over the subcontinent, and they let fall torrents of rain, day after day. Indoors a **patina** of moisture coats everything, clothes will not dry, and head colds make one miserable. Outside, the city struggles with its everyday routines. Suburban trains do not run, their tracks submerged under feet of muddy water. City drains, routinely untended and choked with tons of garbage, refuse to do their work. Housing colonies turn into **archipelagos.** Mosquitoes assume fearsome proportions.

squalls: sudden violent gusts of wind

patina: a gloss or layer

archipelagos: a group of small islands

4   By August, the monsoon has dulled the world. Trees appear a uniform drab green, the sea stays gray and forbidding, and the city stinks. When, in September, the rains have at last weakened into ineffectual evening drizzles, one is relieved.

5   The monsoon season has, I discovered, a rhythm that the mind and body grow accustomed to. In Dubai last June, when the temperature reached 48° Celsius, I would catch myself glancing at the sky, wondering idly if there was a hint of interesting cloud. My rational self knew there could not be a monsoon here, but the subconscious would not be denied. Some mornings I would awake in my darkened, air-conditioned room and imagine rain drumming on the window. It was an illusion that persisted several seconds into wakefulness, and even after I rose I would resist drawing the curtain aside, preferring instead to retreat to the even darker bathroom. Then I'd tell myself there is no rain, and I'd lace my shoes and step outside into the pitiless heat of Arabia.

6   Late in July, I noticed that the illusions persisted at work, too. With the window blinds down and the central air-conditioning humming along at a cool 22° Celsius, I occasionally caught myself wondering whether I'd find a cab that would be willing to drive me home in the rain. After all, it must be raining outside by now. At these times it took some courage to walk into the passageway between the office suites, face the window, stare at the Dubai skyline carelessly shimmering in the late evening sun, and remind myself that the monsoon lay on the other side of the Indian Ocean.

7   The sounds of rain would still visit, sometimes surprising, always comforting, while outside Dubai still blazed with heat and light. August slipped into September and as the body readjusted itself, the mind played along. As the Gulf's fall months began, the harsh absence of monsoon faded. I no longer looked for that high and lonely cloud in the sky. The time for rain had passed, and I wondered whether next year my longing would be the same.

PRACTICE 7

1. The writer begins by comparing the monsoon in Bangladesh with the dry climate in Dubai. He places his thesis statement in paragraph 2. Underline the thesis statement.

2. How does the writer describe Dubai? Write some descriptive words and phrases that he uses.

   _____

   _____

   _____

3. How does the writer describe Bombay during the monsoon season? Write some descriptive words and phrases that he uses.

   _____

   _____

   _____

4. What is the dominant impression in Goswami's essay? Circle the best answer.

   a. Joy   b. Tension   c. Homesickness

   d. Anger   e. Despair

5. The writer appeals to more than one sense. Give an example for each type of imagery.

   a. Sight: _____

   _____

   b. Sound: _____

   _____

   c. Smell: _____

   _____

 The Writer's Room   **Topics for Descriptive Essays**

Writing Activity 1

Write a descriptive essay about one of the following topics.

General Topics

1. a celebration
2. a future car or house
3. a painting or photograph
4. a shopping area
5. a physical and psychological self-portrait
6. a train or bus station, or a hospital waiting room

College and Work-Related Topics

7. your first impressions of college
8. relaxing areas on campus
9. a past or current workplace
10. your college or workplace cafeteria or food court
11. a memorable person with whom you have worked
12. a pleasant or unpleasant task

> **PARAGRAPH LINK**
>
> You could also develop one of the topics in Chapter 6, "Description."

Writing Activity 2

Read the following quotations. Find one that you agree or disagree with, or find one that inspires you in some way. Then write a descriptive essay based on the quotation.

> The real voyage of discovery consists not in seeking new landscapes but in having new eyes.
>
> —Marcel Proust, French author

> There is no need to go to India or anywhere else to find peace. You will find that deep place of silence right in your room, your garden, or even your bathtub.
>
> —Elisabeth Kubler-Ross, Swiss author

Speak when you are angry—and you will make the best speech you'll ever regret.

—Laurence J. Peter, American educator and author

All sanity depends on this: that it should be a delight to feel heat strike the skin, a delight to stand upright, knowing the bones are moving easily under the flesh.

—Doris Lessing, British author

Iron rusts from disuse, and stagnant water loses its purity and in cold weather becomes frozen; even so does inaction sap the vigor of the mind.

—Leonardo Da Vinci, Italian artist and inventor

DESCRIPTIVE ESSAY CHECKLIST

As you write your descriptive essay, review the essay checklist on the inside front cover. Also ask yourself the following questions.

Does my thesis statement clearly show what I will describe in the rest of the essay?

Does my thesis statement make a point about the topic?

Does my essay have a dominant impression?

Does each body paragraph contain supporting details that appeal to the reader's senses?

Do I use figurative language (simile, metaphor, or personification)?

PARAGRAPH LINK

For more information about process writing, refer to Chapter 7, "Process."

The Process Essay

A **process** is a series of steps done in chronological order. When you write a process essay, you explain how to do something, how something happens, or how something works. There are two main types of process essays.

1. **Complete a process.** Explain how to complete a particular task. For example, you might explain how to create a sculpture or how to give first aid to a choking victim. Each step you describe helps the reader complete the process.

2. **Understand a process.** Explain how something works or how something happens. In other words, the goal is to help the reader understand a process rather than do a process. For example, you might explain how a law is passed or explain how a previous war began.

The Thesis Statement

The thesis statement in a process essay includes the process you are describing and a controlling idea. In the introduction of a process essay, you should also mention any tools or supplies that the reader would need to complete the process.

topic   controlling idea
Choosing a college <u>requires some careful thinking and planning</u>.

topic   controlling idea
Pregnancy <u>consists of several stages</u>.

> ## Hint   List Specific Steps
>
> You can write a thesis statement that contains a map, or guide, to the details that you will present in your essay. To guide your readers, you could mention the main steps in your thesis statement.
>
> topic   controlling idea
> **It is possible to quit smoking** <u>if you focus on your goal</u>, <u>find alternative relaxing activities</u>, and <u>enlist the support of friends and family</u>.

The Supporting Ideas

The body paragraphs in a process essay should explain the steps in the process. Each body paragraph should include details and examples to explain each step.

> ## Hint   Using Commands
>
> When writing a "complete a process" essay, you can use commands when you explain each step in the process. It is not necessary to write *you should*.
>
> command
> First, **introduce** yourself to your roommate.
>
> command
> **Ask** your roommate about his or her pet peeves.

A Process Essay Plan

Read the next essay plan and answer the questions that follow.

Introduction
Thesis statement: By introducing yourself, joining groups, and organizing events, you will have a better chance of making friends in a new neighborhood.

I.   Introduce yourself to your neighbors.
    A. Find a good moment.
    B. Explain that you are new to the neighborhood.
    C. Ask a few questions about the area.
II. Have an outdoor party and invite your neighbors.
    A. Find a pretext (holiday, birthday).
    B. Keep the party casual (the point is to have a relaxing time).
    C. Do not worry if some neighbors turn you down.
    D. Aim to find at least one good friend in your area.

(continued)

III. Get involved in your community.
    A. Volunteer to work at the library.
    B. Become politically active in local elections.

Conclusion: With a bit of effort, you can make friends in any neighborhood.

PRACTICE 8

1. What kind of process essay is this? Circle the best answer.

    a. Complete a process   b. Understand a process

2. Add another supporting idea to body paragraph 3.

_____

_____

3. What organizational method does the writer use? Circle the best answer.

    a. Time   b. Space   c. Emphatic

A Process Essay

In the next essay, Jake Sibley, a musician who maintains an online music site, explains how to become a successful musician. Read the essay and answer the questions.

Steps to Music Success

1   Before you can achieve anything, you must first imagine it. If you are serious about becoming a successful musician, it will serve you well to be looking not only at the next step, but also looking down the road to where you ultimately want to be. There is no question that regularly revisiting the fundamentals is critical to success in any long-term **endeavor.** With that in mind, there are some basic things to consider while pursuing your musical dreams.

endeavor: attempt

2   First, setting specific goals and giving them regular attention is **vital** to achieving success at any level. Goals give direction to your action. Furthermore, achieving goals is a tasty reward that will build your esteem and motivate you to reach even higher. So pick your endpoint, and then write down the steps to get there. If you are just beginning in music, then resolve to take lessons. If you are taking lessons, then resolve to get in a performing band. If you are already performing, then resolve to join a paid project. There is no reason that can keep you from reaching your dream. You just have to plan it and then do it.

vital: extremely important

3   It is also important to spend time, not money, on your dream. Most likely you have seen rookie musicians with stacks of absurdly expensive gear. Certainly I am guilty of walking into a music store and **ogling** the top-end instruments, convinced that if I could afford that equipment, my sound would improve by leaps and bounds: "If I had that guitar, I would practice *every day*." If you are not practicing every day already, a new guitar won't change that. The only investment that will improve your success as musicians is *time*— time spent practicing, time spent learning, and time spent pursuing your goals. The lure of expensive gear is a tempting but false road to better musicianship.

ogling: staring at with desire

4   Furthermore, if you really want to improve, play with others. Music is a form of conversation between human beings. It may well be the oldest language, used for millennia by musically inclined people to jointly convey their own rage, sorrow, hope, and joy to other human beings. Learning music without this community is as futile as learning to play football by yourself. Although hours spent alone with your instrument are certainly necessary for success, engaging in musical conversations and performances is an equally vital element to your progress. A very common weakness among amateur musicians is their inability to make music with other artists—a flaw that can be easily remedied with experience. Even if you are a beginner, get out and play with others and stage a few performances if you can. Without even realizing it, you will begin to assimilate fundamental lessons about listening, interacting, and performing in a live setting that are critical to your future success.

5   Finally, practice, practice, practice! There is simply no other way to ensure your own progress as a musician. Have you been spending hours on the Internet, combing for information on how to market your music, or cheaply record a CD, or win a music competition? That's great, but have you been spending as least as much time alone with your instrument? If not, you should reconsider your priorities. If you are not practicing several times a week at least, the music you market, or record cheaply, or submit to a competition is not going to get very far. As a musician seeking success at any level, practicing your instrument should be your number-one priority.

6   If you're serious about music, keep focused on your goal. Take the time to learn your craft, and share your gift with others. Do not let anyone else hold you back from what you know you can achieve.

PRACTICE 9

1. Underline the thesis statement of the essay.

2. What type of process essay is this? Circle the best answer.
    a. Complete a process
    b. Understand a process

3. In process essays, the support is generally a series of steps. List the steps to music success.

    _____

    _____

    _____

    _____

4. What organizational method does the author use?
    a. Time order   b. Emphatic order   c. Space order

5. Write down the transitional expressions that Sibley uses to introduce each new paragraph.

    _____

    _____

6. Who is the audience for this essay? _____

7. How could this essay have relevance for people who never play music?

_____

_____

 The Writer's Room **Topics for Process Essays**

PARAGRAPH LINK

You could also develop one of the topics in Chapter 7, "Process."

Writing Activity 1

Write a process essay about one of the following topics.

General Topics

1. how to be happy
2. how to be healthy
3. how to learn a new language
4. how to find a good roommate
5. how something works
6. how to deal with a problematic teenager

College and Work-Related Topics

7. how to manage your time
8. how education can change lives
9. how to plan a project
10. how to do your job
11. how to get ahead in your job
12. how to find satisfaction in your work life

Writing Activity 2

Read the following quotations. Find one that you agree or disagree with or one that inspires you in some way. Then write a process essay based on the quotation.

> Treat the earth well. It was not given to you by your parents; it was loaned to you by your children.
>
> —Native American proverb

> If you judge people, you have no time to love them.
>
> —Mother Teresa, Catholic nun

> Know how to listen, and you will profit even from those who talk badly.
>
> —Plutarch, ancient Greek philosopher

> Every child is an artist. The problem is how to remain an artist once he [or she] grows up.
>
> —Pablo Picasso, Spanish artist

> If you can spend a perfectly useless afternoon in a perfectly useless manner, you have learned how to live.
>
> —Lin Yutang, Chinese author

PROCESS ESSAY CHECKLIST

As you write your process essay, review the essay checklist on the inside front cover. Also ask yourself the following questions.

Does my thesis statement make a point about the process?

Does my essay explain how to do something, how something works, or how something happened?

Do I include all of the steps in the process?

Do I clearly explain the steps in the process or in the event?

Do I mention any tools or equipment that my readers need to complete or understand the process?

The Definition Essay

A definition tells you what something means. When you write a **definition essay,** you give your personal definition of a term or concept. Although you can define most terms in a few sentences, you may need to offer extended definitions for words that are particularly complex. For example, you could write an essay or even an entire book about the term *love*. The way that you interpret love is unique, and you would bring your own opinions, experiences, and impressions to your definition essay.

PARAGRAPH LINK

For more information about definition writing, refer to Chapter 8, "Definition."

The Thesis Statement

In your thesis statement, indicate what you are defining, and include a definition of the term. Look at the three ways you might define a term in your thesis statement.

1. **Definition by synonym.** You could give a synonym for the term.

   term   +   synonym
   Some consumers insist that Frankenfood, or genetically modified food, be labeled.

2. **Definition by category.** Decide what larger group the term belongs to, and then determine the unique characteristics that set the term apart from others in that category.

   term   +   category   +   detail
   A groupie is a fanatical devotee of a musician or band.

3. **Definition by negation.** Explain what the term is not, and then explain what it is.

   term   +   what it is not   +   what it is
   Stalkers are not misguided romantics; they are dangerous predators.

The Supporting Ideas

In a definition essay, you can support your main point using a variety of writing patterns. For example, in a definition essay about democracy, one supporting paragraph could give historical background about democracy, another could include a description of a functioning democracy, and a third paragraph could compare different styles of democracy. The different writing patterns would all support the overriding pattern, which is definition.

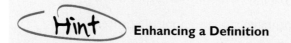 **Enhancing a Definition**

One way to enhance a definition essay is to begin with a provocative statement about the term. Then in the body of your essay, develop your definition more thoroughly. This technique arouses the interest of the readers and makes them want to continue reading. For example, the next statement questions a common belief.

According to Dr. W. Roland, attention deficit disorder is an invented disease.

A Definition Essay Plan

Read the next essay plan and answer the questions that follow.

Introduction

Thesis statement: Depression is not just the blues; it is a serious health problem.

I. A depressed person cannot just "snap out of it."
    A. is not a sign of self-indulgence
    B. some people battle the illness for years and need specific treatment
    C. offer the example of Katie Rowen, who has been hospitalized several times
    D. quotations from people suffering from depression: William Styron says, "Nightfall seemed more somber"; Mike Wallace calls it "endless darkness"

II. Symptoms are not always obvious and can be overlooked.
    A. excess fatigue, lack of energy
    B. unexplained bouts of sadness
    C. extremely irritable for no obvious reason
    D. academic and work performance suffer

III. Depression has impacts on a person's physical and emotional life.
    A. may neglect nutrition, leading to excess weight gain or weight loss
    B. may neglect appearance and hygiene
    C. may alienate family and co-workers
    D. may suffer job loss, leading to financial consequences

Conclusion: Depression is a serious illness that affects many people in our society.

PRACTICE 10

1. What type of definition does the writer use in the thesis statement? Circle the best answer.
    a. Definition by synonym   b. Definition by category
    c. Definition by negation

2. The writer uses many types of supporting details. Underline a quotation, and circle an anecdote.

3. What organizational strategy does the writer use? Circle the best answer.
   a. Time order   b. Emphatic order   c. Space order

A Definition Essay

In the next essay, student writer Diego Pelaez defines a sports fanatic. Read the essay and answer the questions.

Sports Fanatics

1   The opposing team's greatest player received the ball with time running low. His team down a point, he went to work on his defender. Faking a rush to the basket, he stepped back and rose for the deciding jump shot of the game. He released the ball with a good arc, and sure enough, it found its target, winning the game and the championship. I watched silently and shared the sorrow of the team, for I am a sports fanatic. When a beloved team loses, the true sports fanatic feels like he or she has been through a personal tragedy. For sports fanatics, the game is not just a game; it is one of life's most significant events.

2   Sports fanatics never hesitate to show devotion to the team, for devotion is what separates a true sports fanatic from the average, casual sports fan. The casual fan may express **complacency** when the team loses. A sports fanatic feels each defeat with stretches of sorrow and answers each victory with **jubilation.** When my team lost that championship game, I was **despondent** for over a week. I kept going over the game in my head, imagining what might have happened had the game ended a few seconds earlier.

> **complacency:** contentment
>
> **jubilation:** extreme joy
>
> **despondent:** miserable

3   Statistics are a vital part to the full understanding of any sport, and sports fanatics know this fact. Fanatics learn everything that they can about the game. They can usually rattle off at least a few statistics that can make regular people question their use of their spare time. Yet despite the opinions of others, true sports fans wear their ability to memorize statistics as a badge of honor and as proof of their undying dedication. For example, when I meet a fellow fanatic, I excitedly recite numbers, names, and dates, often competing to show that I have amassed more information about my favorite sport than others.

4   True sports fanatics are not crazy; they simply have an **avid** fantasy life. Millions of kids imitate Joe Montana or Michael Jordan, dreaming of becoming a major leaguer. Even if the sports fanatic is a poor player, he or she has usually played the game in order to fully understand the sport. In essence, the thrill of the sports fanatic is to **live vicariously** through the people talented enough to achieve the fanatic's childhood dreams. I spend many pleasurable moments imagining that I can hear the roar of the crowd when I make that winning jump shot.

> **avid:** full, enthusiastic
>
> **live vicariously:** to imagine participating in someone else's experience

5   The sports fanatic is a hard creature to understand. Others may wonder why die-hard fans care so much about sports. The point is, fanatics have a purpose in life: they truly care about something, and they express their devotion wholeheartedly. Some of the greatest athletes are sports fanatics too. Growing up, Michael Jordan was passionate about baseball and basketball. Wayne Gretzky spent his childhood absorbing everything that he could about hockey. So instead of regarding sports fanatics as crazy, people should commend them for their commitment and love of the game.

PRACTICE 11

1. Underline the thesis statement of the essay.

2. What introduction style does the writer use in this essay? Circle the best answer.

   a. Anecdote   b. Historical information   c. Shocking statement

3. In paragraph 2, the writer compares a fanatic with a casual fan. What is the main difference between the two?

   _____

   _____

4. Using your own words, list the main supporting ideas in this essay.

   a. _____

   b. _____

   c. _____

5. Look in the essay, and find an example of definition by negation. Write it here.

   _____

   _____

6. What method does the writer use to end this essay? Circle the best answer.

   a. Quotation   b. Suggestion   c. Prediction

The Writer's Room   Topics for Definition Essays

PARAGRAPH LINK

You could also develop one of the topics found in Chapter 8, "Definition."

Writing Activity 1

Write a definition essay about one of the following topics.

General Topics

1. propaganda
2. a pacifist
3. street smarts
4. a control freak
5. a blog
6. a generation gap

College and Work-Related Topics

7. a McJob
8. a perfectionist
9. a whistle-blower
10. an ineffective boss
11. affirmative action
12. downsizing

Writing Activity 2

Read the following quotations. Find one that you agree or disagree with, or find one that inspires you in some way, and use it as the basis for a definition essay.

A cult is a religion with no political power.

—Tom Wolfe, American author

Tact is the ability to describe others as they see themselves.

—Abraham Lincoln, former American president

One of the keys to happiness is a bad memory.

—Rita Mae Brown, American activist

A leader who does not hesitate before he sends his nation into battle is not fit to be a leader.

—Golda Meir, former Israeli prime minister

Opportunity is missed by most people because it is dressed in overalls and looks like work.

—Thomas A. Edison, American inventor

DEFINITION ESSAY CHECKLIST

As you write your definition essay, review the essay checklist on the inside front cover. Also ask yourself the following questions.

☐ Does my thesis statement explain what term I am defining?

☐ Does each topic sentence clearly show some aspect of the definition?

☐ Do my supporting paragraphs include examples that help illustrate the definition?

☐ Do I use concise language in my definition?

The Classification Essay

Classifying means "to sort a subject into more understandable categories." When you are planning a classification essay, find a topic that you can divide into categories. Each of the categories must be part of a larger group, yet they must also be distinct. For example, if your essay is about types of lawyers, you might sort them into criminal lawyers, divorce lawyers, and corporate lawyers.

> **PARAGRAPH LINK**
>
> For more information about classification writing, refer to Chapter 9, "Classification."

The Thesis Statement

The thesis statement in a classification essay mentions the categories of the subject and contains a controlling idea. In this type of essay, the controlling idea is your classification principle, which is the overall method that you use to sort the items. For example, if your essay topic is "children," you might sort them according to their stages of development, their birth order, or their social classes.

controlling idea (classification principle)   topic
<u>Birth order has a profound influence on</u> **the personalities of children.**

> ⟨**Hint**⟩ **List Specific Categories**
>
> You can guide your reader by listing the specific categories you will cover in your thesis statement.
>
>   topic   controlling idea
> **Children learn gender roles** through the family, the school, and the media.

The Supporting Ideas

In a classification essay, each body paragraph covers one category. To organize your categories and supporting details, you can use a classification chart or a more traditional classification essay plan.

A Classification Chart

A classification chart helps you plan your ideas by providing a visual representation of how you wish to classify a subject. In this sample chart, the thesis statement appears at the top, and all of the categories branch from it.

Historically, three types of marital unions have been practiced around the world.

Monogamy	Polygyny	Polyandry
- marriage between one man and one woman - most commonly accepted - because of divorce, some practice serial monogamy	- males may have more than one wife - common in preindustrial societies - practiced today by some religious groups	- females may have more than one husband - was common in some tribal societies in India - rare to nonexistent today

A Classification Essay Plan

A classification essay plan also helps you organize your essay's categories and details. Read the next essay plan and answer the questions.

Introduction
Thesis statement: There are three main types of bad jokes: overused children's jokes, practical jokes, and insulting jokes.

I. Overused children's jokes bore the listener.
    A. knock-knock jokes
    B. "what is it" jokes
    C. "why did the chicken cross the road" jokes
    D. silly riddles

II. Practical jokes humiliate the victims.
    A. whoopee cushions
    B. plastic wrap on the toilet seat
    C. paint can over the door
    D. "kick me" note on a person's back

III. Insulting jokes can seriously hurt or offend others.
   A. jokes about ethnic groups or religious groups
   B. jokes about a person's appearance (big nose jokes, blond jokes)
   C. jokes about a profession (lawyer jokes)

Conclusion: As long as people laugh at them, bad jokes will continue to be repeated.

PRACTICE 12

1. What is the classification principle? That is, what main principle unifies the three categories?

   _____

2. Why is each type of joke considered bad? Underline the reason in each topic sentence.

3. The author organizes the main ideas in emphatic order. How are they arranged? Circle the best answer.

   a. From most to least offensive   b. From least to most offensive

4. How does the writer support the main ideas? Circle the best answer.

   a. Examples   b. Anecdotes   c. Statistics

A Classification Essay

Read the next essay by student writer Naomi Ihara and answer the questions.

ATM Fraud

1   In the 1980s, automated teller machines started appearing in bank entrances, gas stations, and grocery stores. As fast as the machines appeared, so did criminals who were intent on finding ways to rob the **ATMs.** Today, there are three very effective types of bank machine crimes occurring across the nation: no-tech, low-tech, and high-tech.

ATMs: automated teller machines

2   Criminals who attempt no-tech crimes use simple methods to defraud others. For example, a thief may stand near a bank machine and intently watch people punching in their **PIN** codes. After reading the code, the thief follows the victim and waits for the right moment to attack. Then the thief snatches the victim's purse or wallet in order to get the card. With the debit card and the code, the crook can empty the victim's account. Another method is to look through recycling waste for receipts and bank statements. With a name, birth date, and personal banking information, a thief can steal someone's identity and try to get a new bank card issued in the victim's name. These types of criminals are the most likely to be caught.

PIN: personal identification number

3   Several low-tech methods of defrauding customers exist. One method involves the use of an inexpensive plastic sleeve that is inserted into the debit card slot. Later, after inserting a debit card, the customer attempts to punch in his or her personal identity number. The machine instructs the customer to re-enter the code because it cannot read the automatic strip on the card. The customer, who is being watched, makes several futile attempts and then leaves, assuming the machine has kept the card. A few minutes later,

a criminal removes the sleeve containing the card from the machine, re-enters the card, types in the victim's PIN code, and removes cash. Another low-tech method involves the use of a false cash dispenser cover. A thief removes the cover from one machine and places it on another. When customers attempt to remove cash, the false cover blocks the cash dispenser. Victims leave, assuming the machine has malfunctioned. Then the thief arrives, removes the false cover, and takes the money.

4   High-tech methods include the use of card readers and fake bank machines. The card readers are small devices that can be attached to an ATM machine. Anna C. Irwin, in an article for the Maryville, Tennessee paper, *The Daily Times*, recounts the story of Mike and Roxanne Coffey. They arrived at a machine and read a notice telling them that due to recent fraud attempts, they should use an electronic reader beside the machine. They did so, and then noticed that the reader was not properly attached to the wall. They alerted the bank and were told that the machine was not bank property. Apparently, such card readers give criminals all the data they need to make and use false bankcards. Furthermore, in some areas, police have discovered fake bank machines sitting in entrances to retail outlets. Customers insert their cards into the fake machines, unknowingly giving criminals their card and PIN information.

5   According to the American Bankers Association, banks lose over fifty million dollars per year due to debit card fraud. Although most banks quickly reimburse customers who are victims of such scams, not all do. Some customers report having to fight with bank employees for months over unexplained withdrawals from their accounts. It is always a good idea to be vigilant when using a bank machine. If something seems odd, trust your instincts and report it.

PRACTICE 13

1. Underline the thesis statement of the essay.

2. What is the essay's classification principle? _____

_____

3. The author lists three main categories. What are they?

_____

4. Underline the topic sentences in the body paragraphs.

5. To better understand how the author organizes this essay, make a classification chart. Write the categories on the lines and examples in the boxes.

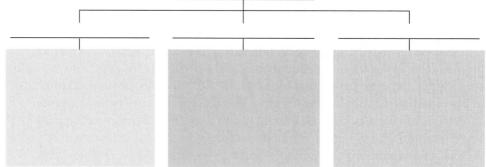

Types of ATM Fraud

The Writer's Room   **Topics for Classification Essays**

Writing Activity 1

Write a classification essay about one of the following topics.

PARAGRAPH LINK

You could also develop one of the topics found in Chapter 9, "Classification."

General Topics

1. addictions
2. transportation
3. extreme sports
4. things that cause allergic reactions
5. youth subcultures
6. punishment

College and Work-Related Topics

7. professions
8. art
9. work-related expenses
10. success
11. conversational topics at work
12. fashions in the workplace

Writing Activity 2

Read the following quotations. Find one that you agree or disagree with, or find one that inspires you in some way. Then write a classification essay based on the quotation.

> Work saves us from three great evils: boredom, vice, and need.
>
> —Voltaire, French author and philosopher

> There are three kinds of lies: lies, damned lies, and statistics.
>
> —Benjamin Disraeli, British politician

> Nothing is particularly hard if you divide it into small jobs.
>
> —Henry Ford, American inventor

> There appears to be three types of politicians: leaders, lobbyists, and professionals.
>
> —R. Ravimohan, Indian journalist

> Never bear more than one trouble at a time. Some people bear three kinds—all they have had, all they have now, and all they expect to have.
>
> —Edward Everett Hale, American author and clergyman

✔ CLASSIFICATION ESSAY CHECKLIST

As you write your classification essay, review the essay checklist on the inside front cover. Then ask yourself the following questions.

☐ Do I clearly identify which categories I will discuss in my thesis statement?

☐ Do I use a common classification principle to unite the various items?

(continued)

Do I include categories that do not overlap?

Do I clearly explain one of the categories in each body paragraph?

Do I use sufficient details to explain each category?

Do I arrange the categories in a logical manner?

PARAGRAPH LINK

For more information about this pattern, refer to Chapter 10, "Comparison and Contrast."

The Comparison and Contrast Essay

You **compare** when you want to find similarities and **contrast** when you want to find differences. When writing a comparison and contrast essay, you explain how people, places, things, or ideas are the same or different to prove a specific point.

Before you write, you must make a decision about whether you will focus on similarities, differences, or both. As you explore your topic, it is a good idea to make a list of both similarities and differences. Later, you could use some of the ideas in your essay plan.

The Thesis Statement

The thesis statement in a comparison and contrast essay indicates if you are making comparisons, contrasts, or both. When you write a thesis statement, indicate what you are comparing or contrasting and the controlling idea.

Although neat people have a very nice environment, messy people are more relaxed.

Topics being contrasted: Neat people and messy people

Controlling idea: Messy people are more relaxed

Alice's daughter wants to be her own person, but she is basically very similar to her mother.

Topics being compared: Mother and daughter

Controlling idea: Very similar personalities

The Supporting Ideas

In a comparison and contrast essay, you can develop your body paragraphs in two different ways.

1. In a **point-by-point** development, you present *one* point about Topic A and then *one* point about Topic B. You keep following this pattern until you have a few points for each topic.

   Point A   Point B   Point A   Point B   Point A   Point B

2. In a **topic-by-topic** development, you discuss one topic in detail, and then you discuss the other topic in detail.

   All of Topic A   All of Topic B

A Comparison and Contrast Essay Plan

Read the next essay plan and answer the questions.

Introduction

Thesis statement: Although I earned a lot when I was an accountant, I am much happier just working in a bank.

I.   When I worked as an accountant, my family life suffered.
   A. Before, I yelled at my children because of stress.
   B. I worked evenings and weekends visiting clients.
   C. I didn't give my spouse any attention.
   D. I didn't take time to do family things.
II. My health was in danger when I was an accountant.
   A. I got panic attacks during tax time.
   B. My blood pressure rocketed when clients yelled at me.
   C. If I made a mistake, I felt physically ill with guilt.
   D. I drank and smoked more to cope with stress.
III. Now in my new bank job, I have less stress and my family life is better.
   A. Now I work only 9 to 5, and no weekends or evenings.
   B. We do family activities every Sunday.
   C. Now my bank clients are happy to see me.
   D. My days are relaxed, and my co-workers are pleasant.
   E. My health is better, and I no longer have panic attacks.

Conclusion: Do not sacrifice your family for your job.

PRACTICE 14

1. The writer compares and contrasts two things in this essay plan. What are they?

   _____

   _____

2. Look at the thesis statement. What is the controlling idea?

   _____

   _____

3. What will this essay focus on? Circle the best answer.
   a. Similarities   b. Differences

4. Look at paragraphs 1 through 3. What comparison and contrast style does the writer use? Circle the best answer.
   a. Point by point   b. Topic by topic

A Comparison and Contrast Essay

In the next essay, college student Emily Hotte compares two eras. Read the essay and answer the questions.

The Unchanging Generation

1   In the 1920s, life was more difficult for most people than it is today. There were no electric washers, dryers, or dishwashers. Racism was more rampant, and so was sexism. Women were expected to work in the home, and few universities accepted female students. Entertainment was different, too. People listened to radios and watched silent films. They did not have televisions, MP3 players, computers, or cellular phones. Yet in spite of these differences, young people in the 1920s were very much like young people today.

2   Today, young people want to be popular, and they go to great lengths to fit in with their friends, yet this was also true in the 1920s. F. Scott Fitzgerald wrote stories and novels that describe the 1920s, and he portrays a world where young people are divided among those who are popular and those who are not. In his short story "Bernice Bobs Her Hair," the main character is a shy, socially awkward girl who feels a "vague pain that she was not at present engaged in being popular" (26). In a desperate effort to make friends, Bernice changes her style and modifies her personality in order to be accepted by her peers. Today's youths also worry about popularity. Those who are not part of the "in" crowd are often ridiculed and rejected, and those at the top of the social hierarchy are imitated, envied, and admired. In several highly publicized cases of school violence, the perpetrators complained of being unpopular outcasts who were bullied by more popular students.

3   Teens of the 1920s, like teens today, tried to distinguish themselves from previous generations. In the 1920s, young "flapper" women stopped wearing corsets; they wore skirts that showed their legs; and, in an act of extreme rebellion, they cut their long hair short. In Fitzgerald's story, Bernice calls bobbed hair on women "immoral" but then notes that "you've either got to amuse people or feed 'em or shock 'em" (21). Today, teenagers also differentiate themselves from their elders in an attempt to forge their own identities and create a sense of independence. To the chagrin of their parents, teens color their hair distinctive shades and tattoo or pierce body parts. Some commentators lament the deplorable state of youth fashion, complaining that their daughters expose too much skin and their sons wear poorly fitting clothing.

4   In contemporary subcultures, music is an element that can bond youths together but enrage parents, and the same was true in the 1920s. Fitzgerald called the 1920s the "Jazz Age" and said that youths were a jazz-nourished generation. Jazz, which was created by African Americans, was noted for its forceful rhythms and improvisations. Many parents associated the music with immoral behavior; however, that did not stop armies of kids from crowding jazz clubs. Today, virtually all youth subcultures identify with a particular music style. Punk, alternative, rap, and hip-hop are just some musical styles associated with various youth groups. Often, the music, with its violent or sexual lyrics, enrages older generations. In fact, in the early 2000s, a Senate subcommittee looked at the impact of violent lyrics on urban youths.

5   Although many things have changed since the 1920s, the characteristics of adolescents have remained fundamentally the same. Rebellious youths in the 1920s attacked social conventions by adopting new and shocking styles and by dancing to music that was considered **licentious.** Today, youths do much the same things. Perhaps the association of youth and rebellion is simply part of the human condition. In fact, about two thousand years ago,

licentious: immoral or shameful

Seneca, a Roman philosopher and statesman, said, "It is a youthful failing to be unable to control one's impulses."

PRACTICE 15

1. Underline the thesis statement of the essay.

2. In the thesis statement, what two things does the writer compare?

   _____

3. What does this essay focus on? Circle the best answer.
   a. Similarities   b. Differences

4. What pattern of comparison does the writer follow in paragraph 2? Circle the best answer.
   a. Point by point   b. Topic by topic

5. Using your own words, list the writer's main supporting points.

   _____

   _____

   _____

6. In the conclusion, how does the quotation support the writer's main point?

   _____

   _____

The Writer's Room   Topics for Comparison and Contrast Essays

Writing Activity 1

Write a comparison and contrast essay about one of the following topics.

General Topics

Compare and/or contrast . . .

1. a liberal and a conservative
2. expectations about parenthood vs. the reality of parenthood
3. two sides of a controversial issue
4. living together and getting married
5. manners today and manners fifty years ago
6. a book and a film about the same topic

College and Work-Related Topics

Compare and/or contrast . . .

7. male and female college athletes
8. working with others and working alone
9. a good manager and a bad manager
10. a stay-at-home parent and an employed parent
11. student life and professional life
12. expectations about a job and the reality of that job

> **PARAGRAPH LINK**
>
> You could also develop one of the topics found in Chapter 10, "Comparison and Contrast."

Writing Activity 2

Read the following quotations. Find one that you agree or disagree with, or find one that sparks your imagination. Then write a comparison and contrast essay based on the quotation.

My grandfather once told me that there are two kinds of people: those who work, and those who take the credit. He told me to try to be in the first group; there was less competition there.

—Indira Gandhi, Indian politician

People are more violently opposed to fur than leather because it is safer to harass rich women than motorcycle gangs.

—Unknown

Happy families are all alike. Every unhappy family is unhappy in its own way.

—Leo Tolstoy, Russian author

Commandments for wives:

1. Don't bother your husband with petty troubles and complaints when he comes home from work.
2. Let him relax before dinner, and discuss family problems after the "inner man" has been satisfied.

Commandments for husbands:

1. Remember your wife wants to be treated as your sweetheart.
2. Compliment her new dress, hair-do, and cooking.

—Edward Podolsky, American author of 1947 self-help manual

The first half of our lives is ruined by our parents, and the second half is ruined by our children.

—Clarence Darrow, American defense lawyer

✔ COMPARISON AND CONTRAST ESSAY CHECKLIST

As you write your comparison and contrast essay, review the essay checklist on the inside front cover. Also ask yourself the following questions.

☐ Does my thesis statement explain what I am comparing or contrasting?

☐ Does my thesis statement make a point about my topic?

☐ Does my essay focus on either similarities or differences?

☐ Does my essay include point-by-point and/or topic-by-topic patterns?

☐ Do all of my supporting examples clearly relate to the topics that are being compared or contrasted?

☐ Do I use transitions that will help readers follow my ideas?

The Cause and Effect Essay

When writing a cause and effect essay, you explain why an event happened or what the consequences of such an event were.

PARAGRAPH LINK

For more information about this pattern, refer to Chapter 11, "Cause and Effect."

The Thesis Statement

The thesis statement in a cause and effect essay contains the topic and the controlling idea. The controlling idea indicates whether the essay will focus on causes, effects, or both.

> topic   controlling idea (causes)
> **Chronic insomnia** is caused by many factors.

> topic   controlling idea (effects)
> **Chronic insomnia** can have a serious impact on a person's health.

> topic   controlling idea (causes and effects)
> **Chronic insomnia,** which is caused by many factors, can have a serious impact on a person's health.

Hint   **Thinking About Effects**

If you are writing about the effects of something, you might think about both the short-term and long-term effects. By doing so, you will generate more ideas for the body of your essay. You will also be able to structure your essay more effectively by moving from short-term to long-term effects.
    For example, look at the short- and long-term effects of a smoke-free work zone.

Short term:	Inside air is cleaner.
	The smokers get more coffee breaks.
Long term:	Fewer smoke-related illnesses occur in nonsmokers.
	Some smokers might quit smoking.

PRACTICE 16

Look at the following thesis statements. As you read each sentence, ask yourself whether it focuses on causes, effects, or both. Circle the best answers.

1. Youths join street gangs because they crave excitement, want to belong to a group, and feel safer in a gang.
   a. Causes   b. Effects   c. Both

2. Now that I am a vegetarian, I have more energy, fewer health problems, and greater self-respect.
   a. Causes   b. Effects   c. Both

3. Because of world demand for wood, meat, and gold, the depletion of natural resources in the Amazon jungle is progressing at an alarming rate.
   a. Causes   b. Effects   c. Both

The Supporting Ideas

The body paragraphs in a cause and effect essay focus on either causes, effects, or both. Make sure that each body paragraph contains specific examples that clarify the cause and/or effect relationship.

A Cause and Effect Essay Plan

Read the next essay plan and answer the questions.

Introduction

Thesis statement: I have become a vegetarian for three important reasons.

I. I cannot justify killing something with a nervous system.
   A. I do not want to hurt living creatures.
   B. Animals with a nervous system suffer horribly when they are killed for food.
   C. Methods used in slaughterhouses are inhumane.

II. A vegetarian diet is healthier than a meat-based diet.
   A. In modern agricultural practices, steroids are given to farm animals.
   B. Meat products have higher cholesterol levels than plant and grain products.
   C. Vegetables and beans ensure an adequate supply of nutrients and proteins.

III. A vegetarian diet is inexpensive.
   A. Vegetables are cheaper than meat.
   B. It is cheaper to produce one pound of vegetables than one pound of beef.
   C. People can grow their own vegetables.

Conclusion: A vegetarian diet is a healthy alternative.

PRACTICE 17

1. In the thesis statement, circle the topic and underline the controlling idea.

2. Does this essay focus on causes or effects? _____

3. Who is the audience for this essay? _____

A Cause and Effect Essay

Read the next essay by student writer Jim Baek and then answer the questions that follow.

Why Small Businesses Fail

1   Last spring, Pablo Ortiz rented a tiny pizzeria in his neighborhood to turn it into a taco restaurant. Full of enthusiasm, he bought supplies, paid for advertisements, and posted a large menu in the window of his new venture, called Taco Heaven. Ten months later, Taco Heaven closed, and Ortiz declared bankruptcy. He was not alone. The Small Business Administration Office

reports that close to half of all new businesses fail within the first five years. Causes of small business failures are numerous.

2   First, inexperienced business owners often neglect to do market research to find out if community members are interested in the product. In Ortiz's case, he thought that area residents would appreciate the chance to buy hearty chicken or pork tacos. However, locals were used to paying $2 for a slice of pizza and were unwilling to spend $3 for a homemade taco.

3   Second, inadequate pricing can hurt new businesses. Maggie Stevens, owner of a successful restaurant in Los Angeles, sells stuffed Belgian waffles to an eager clientele. Before pricing her waffles, she calculated the exact cost of each plate, right down to the strawberry that adorned the waffle and the touch of cream next to it. She also considered other costs beyond that of the ingredients, including the cost of labor and food spoilage. Her final price for each dish was 60 percent higher than her base cost. Ortiz, on the other hand, had absolutely no idea what he really spent to make each taco. He ended up underpricing his product and losing money.

4   Additionally, many small business owners have insufficient funds to run their ventures successfully. According to accountant Louis Polk, most small businesses operate for four years before they break even, let alone actually make money. Therefore, owners need a cash reserve to get through the first slow years. Ortiz, expecting to make a decent profit right away, did not realize that he would have to use up his savings to keep his business afloat.

5   Finally, inexperienced merchants may underestimate the sheer volume of work involved in running a business. Ortiz admits he was very naive about the workload. Taco Heaven had to be open 15 hours a day, 7 days a week. Ortiz also had to shop for ingredients and do the accounting. After months of grueling work and little to no pay, he burned out.

6   People who plan to open small businesses should become informed, especially about potential pitfalls. Inexperience, lack of proper planning, and insufficient funds can combine to create a business failure.

PRACTICE 18

1. Underline the thesis statement of the essay.

2. Does this essay focus on causes, effects, or both? _____

3. Give an example from the essay of the following:

   a. statistic _____

   _____

   b. anecdote _____

   _____

4. Using your own words, list the four supporting points.

   _____

   _____

   _____

   _____

The Writer's Room **Topics for Cause and Effect Essays**

PARAGRAPH LINK

You could also develop one of the topics found in Chapter 11, "Cause and Effect."

Writing Activity 1

Write a cause and effect essay about one of the following topics.

General Topics

Causes and/or effects of . . .

1. a new law or policy
2. stress
3. going to war
4. getting a divorce
5. voting or not voting
6. leaving your home or homeland

College and Work-Related Topics

Causes and/or effects of . . .

7. being a parent and college student
8. taking time off before college
9. having an office romance
10. working with a friend
11. gossiping in the office
12. changing jobs or career paths

Writing Activity 2

Read the following quotations. Find one that you agree or disagree with or one that inspires you in some way, and use it as the basis for a cause and effect essay.

> When a man tells you that he got rich through hard work, ask him, "Whose?"
>
> —Don Marquis, American humorist

> Another possible source of guidance for teenagers is television, but television's message has always been that the need for truth, wisdom and world peace pales by comparison with the need for toothpaste that offers whiter teeth and fresher breath.
>
> —Dave Barry, American author and humorist

> Sometimes when we are generous in barely detectible ways, it can change someone else's life forever.
>
> —Margaret Cho, American comedian

> All human actions have one or more of these seven causes: chance, nature, compulsion, habit, reason, passion, and desire.
>
> —Aristotle, ancient Greek philosopher

> One of the symptoms of an approaching nervous breakdown is the belief that one's work is terribly important.
>
> —Bertrand Russell, British author and philosopher

CAUSE AND EFFECT ESSAY CHECKLIST

As you write your cause and effect essay, review the essay checklist on the inside front cover. Also ask yourself the following questions.

Does my essay clearly focus on causes, effects, or both?

Do I have adequate supporting examples of causes and/or effects?

Do I avoid using faulty logic (a mere asumption that one event causes another or is the result of another)?

Do I use the terms *effect* and/or *affect* correctly?

The Argument Essay

When you write an **argument essay,** you take a position on an issue, and you try to defend your position. In other words, you try to persuade your readers to accept your point of view.

PARAGRAPH LINK

For more information about argument writing, refer to Chapter 12, "Argument."

The Thesis Statement

The thesis statement in an argument essay mentions the subject and a debatable point of view about the subject. Do not include phrases such as *in my opinion, I think,* or *I am going to talk about* in your thesis statement.

controlling idea   topic

<u>Our college needs to provide</u> **a nightly walk-home service for students.**

Hint   **List Specific Arguments**

Your thesis statement can further guide your readers by listing the specific arguments you will make in your essay.

controlling idea   topic   (arguments)   1

<u>Colleges should implement</u> **work terms** to help students acquire job skills,

      2   3

make professional contacts, and earn money for expenses.

The Supporting Ideas

In the body of your essay, give convincing arguments. Try to use several types of supporting evidence.

PARAGRAPH LINK

For more detailed information about types of evidence, see pages 158–159 in Chapter 12, "Argument."

- **Include anecdotes.** Specific experiences or pieces of information can support your point of view.

- **Add facts.** Facts are statements that can be verified in some way. **Statistics** are a type of fact. When you use a fact, ensure that your source is reliable.
- **Use informed opinions.** Opinions from experts in the field can give weight to your argument.
- **Think about logical consequences.** Consider long-term consequences if something does or does not happen.
- **Answer the opposition.** Think about your opponents' arguments, and provide responses to their arguments.

RESEARCH LINK

For more information about doing research, see Chapter 15, "Enhancing Your Writing with Research."

> **Hint** **Quoting a Respected Source**
>
> One way to enhance your essay is to include a quotation from a respected source. Find a quotation from somebody in a field that is directly related to your topic. When you include the quotation as supporting evidence, remember to mention the source.
>
> According to Dr. Tom Houston, co-director of the American Medical Association's SmokeLess States campaign, secondhand smoke "can lead to serious health consequences, ranging from ear infections and pneumonia to asthma."

An Argument Essay Plan

Read the next essay plan and answer the questions.

Introduction

Thesis statement: America should institute longer vacation time for employees.

I. Paid vacations in America are much shorter than they are in other countries.
   A. My friend Jay complains because he has only one week of paid vacation.
   B. According to Perri Capell (*Wall Street Journal*), many American employees get only a one-week vacation during their first year of work.
   C. Most European countries give employees five weeks of vacation time during their first year of work.
   D. My sister lives in London and gets five weeks off each year.
II. Longer vacations allow employees to have a family life.
   A. Employees with children need time for the children.
   B. With current rules, many children must spend the summer in day camps.
   C. One week is not enough time to have adequate family holidays.
III. Employees with too little time off may burn out.
   A. According to psychologist Brenda Armour, "employees face stress-related illnesses because they don't get enough time off."
   B. Add anecdote about Ted M., who had a nervous breakdown.
   C. The physical health of employees goes down when they lack vacation time.

Conclusion: To improve the health and the morale of employees, the government needs to legislate more leisure time.

PRACTICE 19

1. Circle the topic and underline the controlling idea in the thesis statement.

2. The author uses many types of supporting material.
   a. Underline three anecdotes.   b. Circle two informed opinions.

3. Write a few lines that could appear in the introduction before the thesis statement. (For ideas about how to write an introduction, look in Chapter 13, "Writing the Essay.")

_____

_____

_____

_____

An Argument Essay

In the next essay, student writer Adela Fonseca argues that junk e-mail is a serious problem needing attention from government officials. Read the essay and answer the questions.

Ban Spam

1   Like most young people, I grew up with a mouse between my fingers. I have used computers almost since I could talk. In the early years of the Internet, I received the odd piece of junk mail, and it was not a big deal to erase one or two spams a month. During the last few years, though, it is as if junk-mail salespeople have hijacked the information highway. Where once there were two or three junk e-mails, there are now, literally, billions. They clog the arteries of my Internet highway, **obscuring** legitimate mail. Spam continues to grow at an alarming rate. Although the U.S. government has enacted some legislation aimed at dealing with spam, it has not stopped the problem. Spam is a global problem, and it needs a global solution. Governments need to work together and severely punish those who send junk e-mail because spam is irritating, offensive, and time-consuming.

obscuring: making unclear

2   First of all, spam is incredibly annoying. In the past, the e-mail inbox was a personal world where people could communicate with family and friends. Now it is like a minefield. For example, college student Eric Chu says that when he returned home after spending a week on vacation, he immediately checked his e-mail and found over eighty messages in his inbox. Chu knew that most of the mail would be pure junk. "I scanned the headings and deleted them, one by one. Most of the junk mail had fake sender names like 'Marie' or 'Gail,' and I almost deleted a message from an old friend who had found me," he says. Once upon a time most people looked forward to opening their e-mail boxes. Now many do so with a feeling of frustration and helplessness.

3   Furthermore, the **abundance** of spam is not harmless; in fact, a lot of junk e-mail is offensive. According to Odin Wortman of Internet Working Solutions, about thirty percent of spam is pornographic. Children and older people open such mail hoping for a message from a friend, only to see an offensive picture. Another thirty percent of junk e-mail advertises fraudulent schemes to get rich quick and hawks products of questionable value or safety.

abundance: a lot of something, a good supply

4   Some people say that it is not a big deal to press the delete button. What they forget is that spam consumes a lot of personal and company resources. Some individuals pay hourly rates for phone services and the Internet, and they waste money sifting through spam. Across the country, office employees spend too much time deleting junk mail. Internet providers invest in expensive filtering software to plug holes that let spammers in, but most filtering software is not that effective. It is like trying to block a hole the size of Kansas with a pencil. If nothing is done about the problem, then in the future we may have to delete thousands of junk e-mails each week.

5   Ultimately, spam is annoying, offensive, time-consuming, and expensive. There is nothing good to say about it. Spam marketers will argue that we get junk in our mail, and that cannot be denied, but we do not get crates of junk mail every week. If we did, paper junk mail would be banned in a hurry. The only real solution is for governments around the world to work together to make spam production illegal. Governments must actively hunt down and prosecute spammers.

PRACTICE 20

1. Underline the thesis statement of the essay.

2. What introductory styles open this essay? Circle the best answer.
   a. Definition and anecdote
   b. Anecdote and general information
   c. General information and definition
   d. Historical background information

3. The thesis statement maps out the writer's main arguments. What are her three main arguments?

   _____

   _____

4. Underline the topic sentence in each body paragraph.

5. In the introduction, how does the author show that there is a problem?

   _____

   _____

   _____

6. Find an example in the essay for each of the following types of evidence.
   a. Statistic: _____

   _____

   b. Anecdote: _____

   _____

   c. Logical consequence: _____

   _____

d. Answer to the opposition: _____

_____

7. What are some transitional expressions that the writer uses?

_____

8. With what does the writer conclude her essay? Circle the best answer.
   a. Prediction   b. Quotation   c. Suggestion

The Writer's Room   Topics for Argument Essays

PARAGRAPH LINK

You could also develop one of the topics found in Chapter 12, "Argument."

Writing Activity 1

Write an argument essay about one of the following topics. Remember to narrow your topic and follow the writing process.

General Topics

1. state-sponsored gambling
2. beauty contests
3. gun control
4. an unfair law
5. war
6. the health-care system

College and Work-Related Topics

7. outsourcing of jobs
8. great reasons to choose your college
9. the cost of a university education
10. student activism
11. the retirement age
12. dress codes at work

Writing Activity 2

Read the following quotations. Find one that you agree or disagree with or one that inspires you in some way, and use it as the basis for an argument essay.

Advertising is legalized lying.

—H. G. Wells, British author

An eye for an eye leads to a world of the blind.

—Mahatma Gandhi, Indian activist

Peace is not merely a distant goal that we seek, but the means by which we arrive at that goal.

—Dr. Martin Luther King, Jr., American civil rights leader

The thing that impresses me the most about America is the way that parents obey their children.

—King Edward VIII, British monarch

Choice has always been a privilege of those who could afford to pay for it.

—Ellen Frankfort, American journalist

ARGUMENT ESSAY CHECKLIST

As you write your argument essay, review the essay checklist on the inside front cover. Also ask yourself the following questions.

- Does my thesis statement clearly state my position on the issue?

- Do I include facts, examples, statistics, logical consequences, or answers to my opponents in my body paragraphs?

- Do my supporting arguments provide evidence that directly supports each topic sentence?

- Do I use transitions that will help readers follow my ideas?

Enhancing Your Writing with Research

> " *Research is formalized curiosity. It is poking and prying with a purpose.* "
>
> —Zora Neale Hurston
> *American playwright and author (1891–1960)*

When we want to seek more information about something, we might talk to other people, look for resources in libraries, bookstores, and museums, or search the Internet. You can use the same tools when looking for details to include in your writing.

What Is Research?

When you **research,** you look for information that will help you better understand a subject. For example, when you plan to see a movie and you read movie reviews in the newspaper, you are engaging in research to make an informed decision. At college, you are often asked to quote outside sources in your essays. And, if you have ever looked for a job, you might have read the newspaper's classified ads, talked to employment counselors, or spoken to potential employers.

This chapter gives you some strategies for researching information and effectively adding it to your writing.

Research for Academic Writing

There is a formal type of writing called the research paper. However, many types of academic essays, especially those with the purpose of persuading, can benefit from research. Additional facts, quotations, and statistics can back up your arguments.

OCTAVIO'S PARAGRAPH WITHOUT RESEARCH

Student writer Octavio Sanchez prepared an argument for an essay about circus animals. His purpose was to persuade the reader that large animals should not be used in circuses.

> Large circus animals are a danger to the public and to entertainers. In some circuses, elephants have gone on rampages and attacked or even killed others. Tigers have turned on trainers. After such attacks happen, people wonder why the animal suddenly turned wild. Wild animals are not meant to be performing pets.

Octavio's paragraph, although interesting, is not entirely convincing. He refers to animal attacks but gives no evidence of them, and without references to specific incidents, the reader may be skeptical about his claims. Octavio decided to do some research and add quotations to his paragraph. He found many Internet sites about his topic that are run by animal-rights organizations, but he worried that his readers might be skeptical if he used those sources. He kept searching and found a government Web site with the title "Captive Elephant Accident Prevention Act." He also found information on the U.S. Department of Labor Web site in an article called "Dangerous Jobs." Octavio added this information to his paragraph.

OCTAVIO'S PARAGRAPH WITH RESEARCH

Octavio added an example of an elephant that went on a rampage. ➤

Octavio offered a statistic from a trustworthy source. ➤

Octavio cited a well-known incident that illustrates his point. ➤

> Large circus animals are a danger to the public and to entertainers. In some circuses, elephants have gone on rampages and attacked or even killed others. According to the government House Committee Web site, "In Palm Bay, Florida in 1992, an elephant named Janet went on a rampage while carrying children on her back" ("Captive"). Furthermore, according to the Bureau of Statistics for the U.S. Department of Labor, elephant trainers have a hazardous job, and "the relative risk is 68 times greater than for the typical worker" ("Dangerous"). Elephants are not the only dangerous circus animals. In 2003, the well-publicized tiger attack on Roy Horn, of Sigfried and Roy fame, indicates that even a highly trained and pampered tiger can be volatile. Wild animals are not meant to be performing pets.

Evaluate Sources

Today's technological advances in both print and electronic publishing make it easier than ever to access information. To find information, you can try any of these strategies.

- Look in magazines, encyclopedias, periodicals, and books written by experts.
- Ask a librarian to help you locate information using various research tools, such as online catalogues, CD-ROMs, and microforms.
- Search the Internet by plugging in key words about your topic and allowing a search engine to find related Web sites.

Hint   **Evaluate Internet Sources**

The Internet is a valuable research tool. Many important magazines and newspapers publish on the Internet. However, be careful when you use Internet sources. Some sites contain misleading information, and some sites are maintained by people who have very strong and specific biases. Remember that the content of Internet sites is not always verified for accuracy.

  When you find a source, ask yourself the following questions.

- Is the information relevant and directly related to my topic?

- Who is the author of the work? Is he or she an expert on the subject?

- Does the author clearly favor one viewpoint over another? Could the author have a financial or personal interest in the issue?

- Is the information current? (Check the date of publication of the material you are considering.)

- On different sites, do different authors supply the same information?

Web Addresses

When you evaluate Internet sites, you can often determine what type of organization runs the Web site by looking at the last three letters of the Uniform Resource Locator (URL) address.

URL Ending	Meaning	Example
.com	Company	www.nytimes.com
.edu	Educational institution	univ.phoenix.edu
.gov	Government	www.irs.gov
.net	Network	www.jobs.net
.org	Organization	www.magazines.org

Keeping Track of Sources

When you find interesting sources, make sure that you record the following information. Later, when you incorporate quotations or paraphrases into your work, you can quickly find the source of the information. (You will learn how to cite sources later in this chapter.)

Book, Magazine, Newspaper	Web Site
Author's full name	Author's full name
Title of article	Title of article
Title of book, magazine, or newspaper	Title of Web site
Publishing information (name of publisher, city, and date of publication)	Date of publication or last printing
Pages used	Date you accessed the site
	Complete Web site address

RESEARCH LINK

To find out more about the MLA and its guidelines, visit the MLA Web site at www.mla.org

 Finding Complete Source Information

Source information is easy to find in most print publications. It is usually on the second or third page of the book, magazine, or newspaper. On many Internet sites, however, finding the same information can take more investigative work. When you research on the Internet, look for the home page to find the site's title. The Modern Language Association (MLA) recommends that you find and cite as much information as is available.

Add a Paraphrase, Summary, or Quotation

To add research to a piece of writing, you can paraphrase it, summarize it, or quote it.

- When you **paraphrase,** you use your own words to present someone's ideas.
- When you **summarize,** you briefly state the main ideas of another work.
- When you **quote,** you either directly state a person's exact words (with quotation marks) or report them (without quotation marks).

All of these are valid ways to incorporate research in your writing, as long as you give credit to the author or speaker.

 **Avoid Plagiarism!**

Plagiarism is the act of using someone else's words or ideas without giving that person credit. Plagiarism is a very serious offense and can result in expulsion from college or termination from work.
    The following actions are examples of plagiarism.

• Buying another work and presenting it as your own

• Using another student's work and presenting it as your own

• Failing to use quotation marks or properly set off an author's exact words

• Using ideas from another source without citing that source

• Making slight modifications to an author's sentences, but presenting the work as your own

To avoid plagiarism, always cite the source when you borrow words, phrases, or ideas from an author. Include the author's name, the title of the work, and the page number (if it is available).

Paraphrasing and Summarizing

Although summarizing and paraphrasing have some similarities, they are not the same thing.

Similarities

When paraphrasing and summarizing, you should do the following:

- **Use your own words.** Do not use words or phrases from the original text. Try to restate the author's words in a new way.
- **Always maintain the original meaning or intent of the author.** Do not use the author's words out of context.
- **Avoid including your own opinions.** A paraphrase and a summary present an author's views. Do not include personal observations.
- **Mention the source.** Identify the author and title of the work.

DIFFERENCES

Paraphrases and summaries have different lengths and content.

- **Length** A paraphrase contains close to the same number of words as the original passage. A summary is much shorter than the original passage.
- **Content** A paraphrase contains the same information as the original piece, but in a restated form. A summary presents a global view and contains only the most important ideas in a restated form.

> **Hint** **Consider Your Audience**
>
> When you decide whether to paraphrase or summarize, think about your audience.
>
> • Paraphrase if your audience needs detailed information about the subject.
>
> • Summarize if the audience needs to know only general information.

PRACTICE I

The next selection, written by Adam Liptak, appeared in the August 24, 2003 edition of the New York Times on page A16. Read the selection, the paraphrase, and the summary, and then answer the questions that follow.

Original Selection

Gerald Sanders, 48, will spend the rest of his life in an Alabama prison because he stole a $16 bicycle. He had a five-year history of burglaries, none of them involving violence, and that record was enough under the state's habitual offender law to require a judge to send him away forever. Since California enacted a law requiring tough sentences for many third offenses in 1994, the trend in many states has been toward long, fixed sentences, even for nonviolent crimes.

Paraphrase

Adam Liptak, in the New York Times, reports that an Alabama citizen who committed a minor crime has been sentenced to life imprisonment. Because of a bicycle theft and a series of previous robberies, Gerald Sanders will die in jail. Following California's lead, Alabama and numerous other states have enacted strict three-strike laws that punish habitual offenders, including those who are not violent (A16).

Summary

Numerous states have followed California's lead and enacted three-strike laws, giving long prison sentences to habitual offenders. This law applies even to those who do not use violence, according to Adam Liptak in the New York Times (A16).

1. In the paraphrase and summary, does the writer express an opinion? _____

2. In the paraphrase and summary, the writer gives three pieces of information about the source. What are they?

_____

_____

_____

_____

_____

_____

 **Hint** **Paraphrasing and Summarizing**

When you paraphrase, do not look at the original document. After you finish writing, compare your version with the original and ensure that you have not used too many words from the original document.

When you summarize, look at the key ideas in the text, and rephrase them using your own words.

PRACTICE 2

Read the following selections and answer the questions. The original selection, written by Martin Seligman, appeared in the APA Monitor on page 97.

Original Selection

Unfortunately it turns out that hit men, genocidal maniacs, gang leaders and violent kids often have high self-esteem, not low self-esteem. A recipe for their violence is a mean streak combined with an unwarranted sense of self-worth. When such a boy comes across a girl or parents or schoolmates who communicate to him that he is not all that worthy, he lashes out.

Summary 1

In the APA Monitor, Martin Seligman says that hit men and genocidal maniacs often have high self-esteem. Their mean streak combines with an unwarranted sense of self-worth, and creates a recipe for violence (97).

1. How does this summary plagiarize the original piece of writing?

_____

_____

_____

_____

Summary 2

Violent youths, like hired assassins and other murderers, often have self-esteem that is too high. Such youths lash out when others question their worthiness.

2. How does this summary plagiarize the original piece of writing?

_____

_____

_____

_____

> **Hint** **Mention Your Source**
>
> When you paraphrase or summarize, remember to mention the name of the author and the title of the publication. If the page number is available, place it in parentheses.

PRACTICE 3

Paraphrase and summarize the original selection. Remember that a paraphrase respects the length and order of the original document, whereas a summary is a very condensed version of the original. The next selection, written by Carol R. Ember and Melvin Ember, appeared on page 239 of their book, Cultural Anthropology.

Original Selection

Religious beliefs and practices are found in all known contemporary societies, and archaeologists think they have found signs of religious belief associated with Homo sapiens who lived at least 60,000 years ago. People then deliberately buried their dead, and many graves contain the remains of food, tools, and other objects that were probably thought to be needed in an afterlife.

Paraphrase: _____

_____

_____

_____

_____

_____

_____

_____

_____

Summary: _____

_____

_____

_____

_____

_____

Quoting Sources

An effective way to support your arguments is to include quotations. Use quotations to reveal the opinions of an expert or to include ideas that are particularly memorable and important. When quoting sources, remember to limit how many you use in a single paper and to vary your quotations by using both direct and indirect quotations.

Direct and Indirect Quotations

A **direct quotation** contains the exact words of an author, and the quotation is set off with quotation marks.

> A survey released by the Police Foundation states, "There are enough guns in private hands to provide every adult in America with one."

An **indirect quotation** keeps the author's meaning but is not set off by quotation marks.

A survey released by the Police Foundation states that there are so many privately owned guns in the United States that every adult could be given one.

How to Introduce or Integrate a Quotation

Quotations should be integrated into sentences. To learn how to introduce or integrate quotations in your writing, read the following original selection and then view three common methods. The selection, written by John E. Farley, appeared on page 97 of his book, Sociology.

Original Selection

Human history abounds with legends of lost or deserted children who were raised by wild animals. Legend has it, for example, that Rome was founded by Romulus and Remus, who had been raised in the wild by a wolf.

1. **Phrase introduction** You can introduce the quotation with a phrase followed by a comma. Capitalize the first word in the quotation. Place the page number in parentheses.

    In Sociology, John E. Farley writes, "Human history abounds with legends of lost or deserted children who were raised by wild animals" (97).

    Alternatively, you can place the phrase after the quotation. End the quotation with a comma instead of a period.

    "Human history abounds with legends of lost or deserted children who were raised by wild animals," writes John E. Farley in Sociology (97).

2. **Sentence introduction** Introduce the quotation with a sentence followed by a colon. Capitalize the first word in the quotation.

    In his book Sociology, John E. Farley suggests that such stories are not new: "Human history abounds with legends of lost or deserted children who were raised by wild animals" (97).

3. **Integrated quotation** Integrate the quotation as a part of your sentence. Place quotation marks around the source's exact words. Do not capitalize the first word in the quotation.

    In Sociology, John E. Farley mentions a legend about the twin founders of Rome "who had been raised in the wild by a wolf" (97).

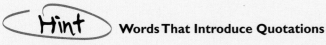 **Words That Introduce Quotations**

One common way to introduce a quotation is to write, "The author says . . ." However, there are a variety of other verbs that you can use.

admits	concludes	mentions	speculates
claims	explains	observes	suggests
comments	maintains	reports	warns

PRACTICE 4

Practice integrating quotations. Read the following selection and then write direct and indirect quotations. The selection, written by Daniel R. Brower appeared on page 371 of his book, The World in the Twentieth Century.

> The collapse of German communism began with the regime's desperate decision to grant complete freedom of travel to East Germans. On the night of November 9, the gates through the Berlin Wall were opened to all. The city became the center of an enormous celebration by East and West Berliners. Some of them climbed the wall itself to celebrate.

1. Write a direct quotation.

   _____

   _____

   _____

   _____

   _____

   _____

2. Write an indirect quotation.

   _____

   _____

   _____

   _____

   _____

   _____

Cite Sources

Each time you use another writer's words or ideas, you must **cite the source,** giving complete information about the original document from which you borrowed the material. You should mention the source both in the body of your work and on a Works Cited page.

> **Hint**   **Choose a Documentation Style**
>
> The three most common styles for documenting sources are the Modern Language Association (MLA) format, Chicago Manual of Style (CMS) format, and the American Psychological Association (APA) format. Before writing a paper, check with your instructor to see which documentation style you should use and to learn where you can find more information about it.

Citing the Source in the Body of Your Essay

When you introduce a quotation or idea, try to mention the source directly in your paragraph or essay. The next few examples show how you can cite some common sources using MLA style.

1. **Mention the author and page number in parentheses.**
Put the author's last name and the page number in parentheses. Place the final period after the parentheses, not inside the quotation marks.

> Successful people fight to succeed: "They have determined that nothing will stop them from going forward" (Carson 224).

2. **Mention the page number in parentheses.**
If you mention the author's name in the introductory phrase, put only the page number in the parentheses. Place the final period after the parentheses.

> "Successful people don't have fewer problems," writes Ben Carson (224).

3. **Mention the Internet site.**
If your source is an Internet site and you do not know the name of the author, place the first word of the site's title in parentheses. Then, remember to write the complete citation on your Works Cited page. Again, place the final period after the parentheses.

> Furthermore, according to the Bureau of Statistics for the U.S. Department of Labor, elephant trainers have a hazardous job, and "the relative risk is 68 times greater than for the typical worker" ("Dangerous").

> ⟨ **Hint** ⟩ **Writing Titles for Borrowed Material**
>
> Place the title of a short work (article or short story) in quotation marks, and underline the title of a longer work (book, magazine, or newspaper). If you are using a computer, you can choose to italicize or underline the titles of longer works.
>
> **Underlined:**   "The End of the Concorde," <u>Vanity Fair</u>
>
> **Italicized:**   "The End of the Concorde," *Vanity Fair*

Preparing a Works Cited Page

Sometimes called a References list or Bibliography, the Works Cited page gives details about each source you have used and appears at the end of your paper. To prepare a Works Cited page, use this format.

- Write Works Cited at the top of the page and center it.
- List each source alphabetically, using the last names of the authors.
- Indent the second line and all subsequent lines of each reference.

Useful Internet Sites

The following Web sites could be useful when you research on the Internet.

Statistics

Statistics from over one hundred government agencies   www.fedstats.gov
Bureau of Labor Statistics   www.stats.bls.gov

News Organizations

Addresses of hundreds of online magazines   newsdirectory.com
Access to newspapers from all over the world   www.newspapers.com
New York Times site for college students   www.nytimes.com/college

Other Sites

Job sites   www.monster.com
                                                            www.jobs.org

Internet Public Library   www.ipl.org/reading
Online encyclopedias   www.encyclopedia.com
                                                            www.britannica.com

Here are some examples of how to cite different types of publications. Notice that the first details are separated by periods, not commas.

Book

■ **One author**

> Last name, First name. "Title of Article." Title of Book. Place of publication: Publisher, Year.

> Tan, Amy. The Joy Luck Club. New York: Random House, 1990.

■ **Two or more authors**

> Ember, Carol R., and Melvin Ember. Cultural Anthropology. New Jersey: Prentice Hall, 2002.

Periodical

■ **Magazine or newspaper**

> Last name, First name. "Title of Article." Title of Magazine or Newspaper Date: pages.

> Foster, Don. "The Message in the Anthrax." Vanity Fair Oct. 2003: 180-200.

■ **Print Journal**

> Last name, First name. "Title of Article." Title of Journal Volume
>   Number. Issue (Year): pages.

> Seligman, Martin. "The American Way of Blame." APA Monitor 29.7
>   (1998): 97.

Internet Site

■ If the information was published on the Internet, include as much of the
following information as you can find. Keep in mind that some sites do not
contain complete information; therefore, you may need to contact the site
administrator to obtain further details.

> Author. "Title of Article." Title of Site or Online Publication. Date of
>   publication. Date you accessed the site <network address>.

> Krystek, Lee. "Crop Circles." Museum of Unnatural Mystery. 2003. 16 May
>   2005 <http://www.unmuseum.org/cropcir.htm>.

■ If the author is not mentioned on the site, begin with the title and include as
much information as you can find. (Note that MLA style does not use periods
with the abbreviation *US*.)

> "Dangerous Jobs." US Department of Labor. 22 July 1997. 28 May 2004
>   <http://stats.bls.gov/iif/oshwc/cfar0020.pdf>.

PRACTICE 5

Imagine that you are using the following sources to write a paper arguing that
athletes can make good role models. Arrange the sources for a Works Cited page.

A quotation

  The quotation is from a magazine article that Alan Paul wrote for
Slam, titled "Unfinished Business." The article, published in the
November 2003 issue, appeared on pages 74 to 78.

A quotation

  The quotation is from a book called American Sports written by
Benjamin G. Rader. The book was published by Prentice Hall, New
Jersey, in 1999.

A paraphrase

The paraphrase is from a Web site titled <u>Muhammad Ali</u>. The text is written by Muhammad Ali. The site at <http://ali.com> was created in 2003 and was accessed on November 28, 2004.

Works Cited

_____

_____

_____

_____

_____

_____

_____

_____

_____

_____

REFLECT ON IT

Think about what you have learned in this chapter. If you do not know an answer, review that topic.

1. What are the differences between a paraphrase and a summary?

   Paraphrase   **Summary**

   _____   _____

   _____   _____

   _____   _____

   _____   _____

2. What are the differences between direct and indirect quotations?

   Direct   **Indirect**

   _____   _____

   _____   _____

   _____   _____

   _____   _____

3. What is a Works Cited page?

   _____

   _____

   _____

   _____

 **The Writer's Room   Research**

Writing Activity 1

Choose a paragraph or an essay that you have written, and research your topic to get more detailed information. Then insert at least one paraphrase, summary, or quotation into your work. Remember to acknowledge your sources.

Writing Activity 2

Write an essay about one of the next topics. Your essay should include research (find at least three sources). Include a Works Cited page at the end of your assignment.

1. Write about a contemporary issue that is in the news. In your essay, give your opinion about the issue.

2. Write about your career choice. You could mention job opportunities in your field, and you could include statistical information.

3. Write about the importance of a college education. Does a college education help or hurt a person's career prospects? Find some facts, examples, or statistics to support your view.

Appendix 1
Grammar Glossary

The Basic Parts of a Sentence

Parts of Speech	Definition	Some Examples
Noun	is a person, place, or thing.	singular: man, dog, person plural: men, dogs, people
Verb	expresses an action or state of being.	action: run, eat, walk, think linking: is, become, seem
Adjective	adds information about the noun.	tall, beautiful, blue, cold
Adverb	adds information about the verb, adjective, or other adverb; expresses time, place, and frequency.	friendly, quickly, sweetly sometimes, usually, never
Pronoun	replaces the noun.	he, she, it, us, ours, themselves
Preposition	shows a relationship between words (source, direction, location, etc.).	at, to, for, from, behind, above
Determiner	identifies or determines if a noun is specific or general.	a, an, the this, that, these, those any, all, each, every, many, some
Coordinating conjunction	connects two ideas of equal importance.	but, or, yet, so, for, and, nor
Subordinating conjunction	connects two ideas when one idea is subordinate (or inferior) to the other idea.	after, although, because, unless, until
Conjunctive adverb	shows a relationship between two ideas. It may appear at the beginning of a sentence, or it may join two sentences.	also, consequently, finally, however, furthermore, moreover, therefore, thus

Types of Clauses and Sentences

Other Key Terms	Definition	Example
phrase	a group of words that is missing a subject, a verb, or both, and is not a complete sentence.	in the morning after the storm
clause	An **independent clause** has a subject and verb and expresses a complete idea.	The movie is funny
	A **dependent clause** has a subject and verb but cannot stand alone. It "depends" on another clause in order to be complete.	Although it is violent
simple sentence	one independent clause that expresses one complete idea.	The movie is funny.
compound sentence	two or more independent clauses that are joined together.	Some movies are funny, and others are deeply moving.
complex sentence	at least one dependent clause joined with one independent clause.	Although the movie is violent, it conveys an important message.
compound-complex sentence	at least two independent clauses joined with at least one dependent clause.	Although the movie is violent, it is very entertaining, and it conveys an important message.

Irregular Verbs

Base Form	Simple Past	Past Participle	Base Form	Simple Past	Past Participle
arise	arose	arisen	feel	felt	felt
be	was, were	been	fight	fought	fought
beat	beat	beat, beaten	find	found	found
become	became	become	flee	fled	fled
begin	began	begun	fly	flew	flown
bend	bent	bent	forbid	forbade	forbidden
bet	bet	bet	forget	forgot	forgotten
bind	bound	bound	forgive	forgave	forgiven
bite	bit	bitten	forsake	forsook	forsaken
bleed	bled	bled	freeze	froze	frozen
blow	blew	blown	get	got	got, gotten
break	broke	broken	give	gave	given
breed	bred	bred	go	went	gone
bring	brought	brought	grind	ground	ground
build	built	built	grow	grew	grown
burst	burst	burst	hang	hung	hung
buy	bought	bought	have	had	had
catch	caught	caught	hear	heard	heard
choose	chose	chosen	hide	hid	hidden
cling	clung	clung	hit	hit	hit
come	came	come	hold	held	held
cost	cost	cost	hurt	hurt	hurt
creep	crept	crept	keep	kept	kept
cut	cut	cut	kneel	knelt	knelt
deal	dealt	dealt	know	knew	known
dig	dug	dug	lay	laid	laid
do	did	done	lead	led	led
draw	drew	drawn	leave	left	left
drink	drank	drunk	lend	lent	lent
drive	drove	driven	let	let	let
eat	ate	eaten	lie*	lay	lain
fall	fell	fallen	light	lit	lit
feed	fed	fed	lose	lost	lost

*When *lie* means "tell a false statement," then it is a regular verb: *lie, lied, lied.*

(continued)

Irregular Verbs (continued)

Base Form	Simple Past	Past Participle	Base Form	Simple Past	Past Participle
make	made	made	speed	sped	sped
mean	meant	meant	spend	spent	spent
meet	met	met	spin	spun	spun
mistake	mistook	mistaken	split	split	split
pay	paid	paid	spread	spread	spread
prove	proved	proved, proven	spring	sprang	sprung
put	put	put	stand	stood	stood
quit	quit	quit	steal	stole	stolen
read	read	read	stick	stuck	stuck
rid	rid	rid	sting	stung	stung
ride	rode	ridden	stink	stank	stunk
ring	rang	rung	strike	struck	struck
rise	rose	risen	swear	swore	sworn
run	ran	run	sweep	swept	swept
say	said	said	swim	swam	swum
see	saw	seen	swing	swung	swung
sell	sold	sold	take	took	taken
send	sent	sent	teach	taught	taught
set	set	set	tear	tore	torn
shake	shook	shaken	tell	told	told
shine	shone	shone	think	thought	thought
shoot	shot	shot	throw	threw	thrown
show	showed	shown	thrust	thrust	thrust
shrink	shrank	shrunk	understand	understood	understood
shut	shut	shut	wake	woke	woken
sing	sang	sung	wear	wore	worn
sink	sank	sunk	weep	wept	wept
sit	sat	sat	win	won	won
sleep	slept	slept	wind	wound	wound
slide	slid	slid	withdraw	withdrew	withdrawn
slit	slit	slit	write	wrote	written
speak	spoke	spoken			

Appendix 3
A Quick Guide to Verb Tenses

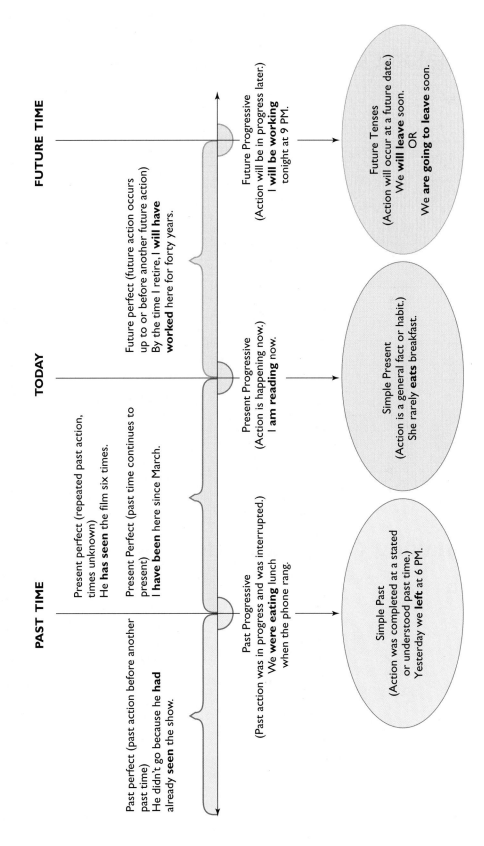

PAST TIME

Past perfect (past action before another past time)
He didn't go because he **had** already **seen** the show.

Present perfect (repeated past action, times unknown)
He **has seen** the film six times.

Present Perfect (past time continues to present)
I **have been** here since March.

Past Progressive
(Past action was in progress and was interrupted.)
We **were eating** lunch when the phone rang.

Simple Past
(Action was completed at a stated or understood past time.)
Yesterday we **left** at 6 PM.

TODAY

Present Progressive
(Action is happening now.)
I **am reading** now.

Simple Present
(Action is a general fact or habit.)
She rarely **eats** breakfast.

FUTURE TIME

Future perfect (future action occurs up to or before another future action)
By the time I retire, I **will have worked** here for forty years.

Future Progressive
(Action will be in progress later.)
I **will be working** tonight at 9 PM.

Future Tenses
(Action will occur at a future date.)
We **will leave** soon.
OR
We **are going to leave** soon.

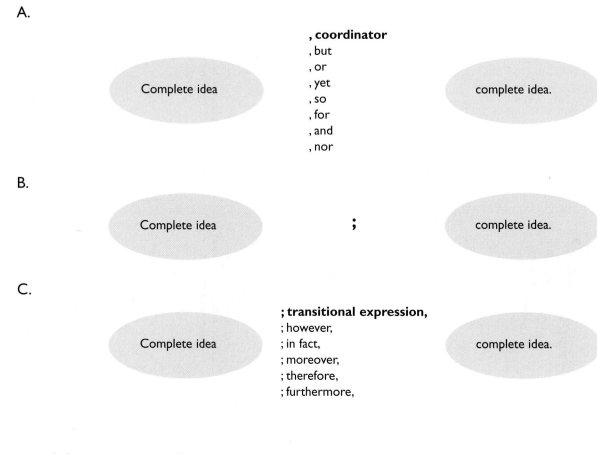

Making Compound Sentences

A.

| Complete idea | **, coordinator**
, but
, or
, yet
, so
, for
, and
, nor | complete idea. |

B.

| Complete idea | ; | complete idea. |

C.

| Complete idea | **; transitional expression,**
; however,
; in fact,
; moreover,
; therefore,
; furthermore, | complete idea. |

Making Complex Sentences

D.

| Complete idea | **subordinator**
although
because
before
even though
unless
when | incomplete idea. |

E.

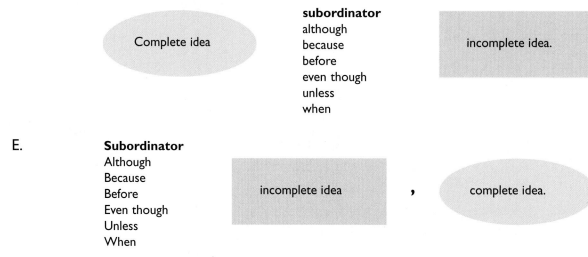

Subordinator
Although
Because
Before
Even though
Unless
When

incomplete idea   ,   complete idea.

Apostrophe (')

Use an apostrophe

- to join a subject and verb together.

    We're late.

- to join an auxiliary with *not*.

    I **can't** come.

- to indicate possession.

    Ross's computer is new.

Comma (,)

Use a comma

- to separate words in a series (more than two things). Place a comma before the final *and*.

    The doctor is kind, considerate, and gentle.

- after an introductory word or phrase.

    In the evenings, Carson volunteered at a hospital.

- around interrupting phrases that give additional information about the subject.

    Alan, an electrician, earns a good salary.

- in compound sentences before the coordinator.

    We worked for hours, and then we rested.

- around relative clauses containing *which*.

    The documents, which are very valuable, are up for auction.

- in quotations, after an introductory phrase or before an ending phrase.

    Picasso said, "Find your passion."

    "Find your passion," Picasso said.

Note: Do not join two complete sentences with a comma!

Colon (:)

Use a colon

- after a complete sentence that introduces a list, or after *the following*.

    The course has the following sections: pregnancy, labor, and lactation.

- after a complete sentence that introduces a quotation.

    Picasso's advice was clear: "Find your passion."

Semicolon (;)

Use a semicolon to join two independent but related clauses.

> Mahatma Gandhi was a pacifist; he believed in nonviolence.

Quotation Marks (" ")

Use quotation marks around direct speech. When a quotation is a complete sentence, capitalize the first word in the quotation. Place the end punctuation inside the closing quotation marks.

> In his essay, Levi said, "We were interchangeable."

If the end of the quotation is not the end of your sentence, end the quotation with a comma. If your quotation ends with other punctuation, put it inside the closing quotation marks.

> "We were interchangeable," according to Levi.
> "You can't be serious!" she shouted.
> "What did you call me?" he replied.

Integrated Quotations

If you integrate a quotation in a sentence, add quotation marks around the words the speaker quoted.

> Dorothy Nixon calls herself a "terrible mother."

"Inside" Quotations

If one quotation is inside another quotation, add single quotation marks (' ') around the inside quotation.

> Bernice was forced to act: "She turned to Charlie Paulson and plunged. 'Do you think I ought to bob my hair?' "

Citing Page or Paragraph Numbers

If you are using MLA style, write the page or paragraph number in parentheses and place it after the quotation. Place the final period *after* the parentheses if the quotation ends the sentence.

> In his essay, Levi says, "We were interchangeable" (4).

Capitalization

Always capitalize

- the pronoun *I* and the first word of every sentence.
- the days of the week, the months, and holidays.

> Tuesday   May 22   Labor Day

- the names of specific places, such as buildings, streets, parks, public squares, lakes, rivers, cities, states, and countries.

> Kelvin Street   Lake Erie   White Plains, New York

- the names of languages, nationalities, tribes, races, and religions.

> Spanish   Mohawk   Buddhist

- the titles of specific individuals.

> **G**eneral **D**ewitt   **D**r. Franklin   **M**r. **B**lain

- the major words in titles of literary or artistic works.

> *The Great Gatsby*   *The Diviners*   *Crime and Punishment*

Punctuating Titles

Place the title of short works in quotation marks. Capitalize the major words. Short works include songs, short stories, newspaper and magazine articles, essays, and poems.

> The Beatles' worst song was "Help."

Underline (or italicize, if you are using a computer) the title of a longer document. Long works include television series, films, works of art, magazines, books, plays, and newspapers.

> We watched the classic movie West Side Story.
> We watched the classic movie *West Side Story*.

Appendix 6
Writing Paragraphs
and Essays in Exams

In many of your courses, you will have to answer exam questions with a paragraph or an essay. These types of questions often allow you to reveal your understanding of the topic. Although taking any exam can be stressful, you can reduce exam anxiety and increase your chances of doing well by following some preparation and exam-writing strategies.

Preparing for Exams

Here are some steps you can take to help prepare for exams.

- Before you take an exam, make sure that you know exactly what material you should study. Do not be afraid to ask the instructor for clarification. Also ask what materials you should bring to the exam.
- Review the assigned information, class notes, and the textbook, if any.
- Read and repeat information out loud.
- Take notes about important points.
- Study with a friend.

Hint **Predict Exam Questions**

An effective study strategy is to predict possible exam questions. Here are some tips:

- Look for important themes in your course outline.
- Study your notes and try to analyze what information is of particular importance.
- Look at your previous exams for the course. Determine whether any questions or subjects are repeated in more than one exam.

After you have looked through the course outline, your notes, and previous exams, write out possible exam questions based on the information that you have collected. Then practice writing the answers to your questions.

Writing Exams

Knowing your material inside and out is a large part of exam writing; however, budgeting your time and knowing how to read exam questions are important, too. When you receive the exam paper, look it over carefully and try these test-taking strategies.

Schedule Your Time

One of the most stressful things about taking an exam is running out of time. Before you write, find out exactly how much time you have. Then, plan how much time you will need to answer the questions. For example, if you have a one-hour exam and you have three questions worth the same point value, try to make sure that you spend no more than twenty minutes on any one question.

Determine Point Values

As soon as you get an exam, scan the questions and determine which questions have a larger point value. For example, you might respond to the questions with the largest point value first, or you might begin with those that you understand well. Then go to the more difficult questions. If you find yourself blocked on a certain answer, do not waste a lot of time on it. Go to another question, and then go back to the first question later.

Carefully Read the Exam Questions

You have probably heard the following anecdote.

> A teacher gave students a test sheet with twenty questions on it. In the instructions at the top of the page, the students were asked to skip to the last question and then hand the test in. Most students did not read the instructions, and they spent a lot of time carefully answering the twenty exam questions.

As this anecdote illustrates, it is important to read the exam instructions thoroughly.

Identify Key Words and Phrases

When you read an exam question, underline or circle key words and phrases in order to understand exactly what you are supposed to do. In the next example, the underlined words highlight three different tasks.

1. Discuss how each time period differs from the other.

Distinguish between Paleolithic, Mesolithic, and Neolithic. Place these periods in chronological order and describe how the people lived during those times.

2. Organize the essay according to each period's date.

3. Discuss what people did for shelter, food, and leisure activities.

Examine Common Question Words

Exam questions direct you using verbs (action words). This chart gives the most common words that are used in both paragraph- and essay-style questions.

Verb	Meaning
describe discuss review	Examine a subject as thoroughly as possible. Focus on the main points.
narrate trace	Describe the development or progress of something using time order.
evaluate explain your point of view interpret justify take a stand	State your opinion and give reasons to support your opinion. In other words, write an argument paragraph or essay.

(continued)

Verb	Meaning
analyze criticize classify	Explain something carefully by breaking it down into smaller parts.
enumerate list outline	Go through important facts one by one.
compare contrast distinguish	Discuss important similarities and/or differences.
define explain what is meant by . . .	Give a complete and accurate definition that demonstrates your understanding of the concept.
explain causes explain effects explain a process summarize illustrate	Analyze the reasons for an event. Analyze the consequences or results of an event. Explain the steps needed to perform a task. Write down the main points from a larger work. Demonstrate your understanding by giving examples.

PRACTICE 1

Determine the main type of response that you would use to answer each essay question.

narrate	explain a process	explain causes/effects	define
argue	classify	compare and contrast	give examples

EXAMPLE:

Discuss the term *affirmative action*.

define

1. Distinguish between the interest rate and the rate of return.

2. Explain what is meant by *democracy*.

3. Describe what happened during the Tet Offensive.

4. List and describe five types of housing.

5. What steps are required to improve your city's transportation system?

6. List the causes of global warming.

_____

7. Give a short but thorough description of narcissism.

_____

8. Briefly explain the differences between a terrorist and a freedom fighter.

_____

9. Discuss whether religious symbols should be banned from schools.

_____

10. Give three instances of how advertising has influenced consumer trends.

_____

Follow the Writing Process

When you answer paragraph or essay exam questions, remember to follow the writing process.

Explore	■ Jot down any ideas that you think can help you answer the question.
Develop	■ Use the exam question to guide your topic sentence or thesis statement.
	■ List supporting ideas. Then organize your ideas and create a paragraph or essay plan.
	■ Write the paragraph or essay. Use transitions to link your ideas.
Revise and edit	■ Read over your writing to make sure it makes sense and that your spelling, punctuation, and mechanics are correct.

PRACTICE 2

Choose three topics from Practice 1 and write topic sentences or thesis statements.

EXAMPLE:
Discuss the term *affirmative action*.

Topic sentence or thesis statement: Affirmative action policies give certain groups in society preferential treatment in order to correct a history of injustice.

1. _____

_____

2. _____

_____

3. _____

_____

PRACTICE 3

Read the following test material and answer the questions that follow.

Essay Exam

You will have ninety minutes to complete the following test. Write your answers in the answer booklet.

A. Define the following terms (2 points each).

1. Region
2. Economic geography
3. Territoriality
4. Spatial distribution
5. Gross national product

B. Write an essay response to one of the following questions. Your essay should contain relevant supporting details. (20 points)

6. Define and contrast an open city with a closed city.
7. Discuss industrial location theories in geography, and divide the theories into groups.
8. Explain the steps needed to complete a geographical survey. List the steps in order of importance.

Schedule Your Time and Determine Point Values

1. What is the total point value of the exam? _____

2. How many questions do you have to answer? _____

3. Which part of the exam would you do first? Explain why. _____

_____

4. Schedule your time. How much time would you spend on each part of the exam?

Part A: _____   Part B: _____

Explain your reasoning. _____

_____

Carefully Read the Exam Questions

5. Identify key words in Part B. What important information is in the instructions?

   _____

6. What two things must you do in question 6?

   a. _____   b. _____

7. What type of essay is required to answer question 7?

   a. Comparison and contrast   b. Classification   c. Process

8. What type of essay is required to answer question 8?

   a. Comparison and contrast   b. Classification   c. Process